SONGS OF MEN

SONGS OF MEN, AN ANTHOLOGY

SELECTED AND ARRANGED BY ROBERT FROTHINGHAM

Fredonia Books
Amsterdam, The Netherlands

Songs of Men, an Anthology

Selected and Arranged
Robert Frothingham

ISBN: 1-4101-0835-X

Copyright © 2005 by Fredonia Books

Reprinted from the 1918 edition

Fredonia Books
Amsterdam, The Netherlands
http://www.fredoniabooks.com

In order to make original editions of historical works available to scholars at an economical price, this facsimile of the original edition of 1918 is reproduced from the best available copy and has been digitally enhanced to improve legibility, but the text remains unaltered to retain historical authenticity.

TO THE WIFE OF MY YOUTH
WHOSE INFLUENCE GROWS
WITH THE YEARS

I have great pleasure in acknowledging my keen appreciation of the hearty and helpful interest of Henry Herbert Knibbs, Walter L. Harden, and Eugene Manlove Rhodes in the compilation of this book of verse.

Robert Frothingham

New York
October, 1918

FOREWORD

Most Kind and Gentle Reader —

If you are looking for old favorites or for something to please the pale æsthetic brow you won't find them here. There's nothing about this collection suggestive of the drawing-room, nothing that by the widest stretch of the imagination could be identified with " his mistress' eyebrow."

Colloquially speaking, this is a bunch of verse intended to appeal to red-blooded men and women. Strong, virile stuff, it sings the Great Outdoors from the Arctic Circle to the Tropics, from the Occident to the Orient. It runs the gamut of man's emotions in-so-far as they can be stimulated by wanderlust, camp and trail, pioneering, seafaring, piracy, sport, battle afloat and ashore, gold-seeking, vagabonds, animals, the Great War, the joy of accomplishment and the bitterness of failure. Our own glorious West is here with its ever-present glamour of mountain peaks, mining camps, cowboys, desert and illimitable plains.

With such an idea in mind as the title indicates, it was inevitable that the old favorites be overlooked and that " many a gem of purest ray serene " should be rescued from obscurity. Yes, and some of them were written by women — not the feminist type which the Great War has swept into the discard, but your real "man's woman" who has a fashion of looking life straight in the eye — and are all the more Songs of Men on that account

Within will be found the first authoritative publication in book form of that famous piratical ditty, "Derelict" or "Fifteen Men on the Dead Man's Chest," elaborated many years ago by my old friend Young Ewing Allison, of Louisville, Kentucky, from Stevenson's renowned quatrain in "Treasure Island," also "The Little Red God," an anonymous bit of verse written especially for this anthology by one of our best-known poets.

On your way, little book.

R. F.

New York
October, 1918

ACKNOWLEDGMENTS

THE editor acknowledges his indebtedness to the following authors and publishers for the use of copyright poems:

Mr. George Matthew Adams for " The Sexton's Inn," from *The Uncle Walt Book*, by Walt Mason.

Messrs. D. Appleton & Co. for " The Last of All," from *Songs of the Stalwart*, by Grantland Rice.

Mr. Richard G. Badger for " The Plainsmen," " The Westerner," and " High-Chin Bob," from *Sun and Saddle Leather*, by Badger Clark.

Messrs. Barse & Hopkins for " The Spell of the Yukon," from *The Spell of the Yukon*, by Robert W. Service.

The Bobbs-Merrill Company for " He does not die," from *The Four Men*, by Hilaire Belloc; " When the Drive goes Down," from *Tote Road and Trail*, by Douglas Malloch.

Mr. Thomas Fleming Day for his poems "Warning," " The Main-Sheet Song," " The Coasters," and " The Sailor of the Sail," from *Songs of Sea and Sail*.

Messrs. George H. Doran Company for " Success," from *In Camp and Trench*, by Berton Braley; "Hastings Mill" and " Shipmates," by Cicely Fox-Smith; " Roofs," from *Trees, and Other Poems*, by Joyce Kilmer; " The Vagabond Grown Old " and " Gipsy-Heart," from *In Deep Places*, by Amelia Josephine Burr.

Messrs. Doubleday, Page & Co. and Mr. Kipling for " The Voortrekker " from *Songs from Books*, and " Beyond the Path of the Outmost Sun," by Rudyard Kipling.

Messrs. Harper & Brothers for " The Road to Vagaboudia," from *Poems*, by Dana Burnet.

Messrs. Houghton Mifflin Company for " The Heart of the Road," from *The Heart of the Road, and Other Poems*, by Anna Hempstead Branch; " This my Life," from *Poems*, by John Vance Cheney; " Out there Somewhere " and " The Walking Man," from *Songs of the Outlands*, and " The Glorious Fool," from *Riders of the Stars*, by Henry Herbert Knibbs; " The Conquest of the Air " and " The Riderless Horse," from *Mothers and Men*, by Harold Trowbridge Pulsifer; " The Klondike," from *Captain Craig: Poems*, by Edwin Arlington Robinson; " Earth-born," " The Singer's Quest," " Wanderlust," and " Whence cometh my Help," from *A Lonely Flute*, by Odell Shepard.

Messrs. P. J. Kenedy & Sons for " The Cry of the Dreamer," from *Selected Poems*, by John Boyle O'Reilly.

Mr. Mitchell Kennerley for " The Green Inn," from *The Joy of Life*, by Theodosia Garrison.

Messrs. John Lane Company for " Impenitentia Ultima," from *Poems*, by Ernest Dowson; " Admirals All " and " Play the Game," from *Admirals All, and Other Verses*, by Henry Newbolt; " An Island Song," from *The Lamp of Poor Souls, and Other Poems*, by Marjorie Pickthall.

Messrs. J. B. Lippincott Company for " The Traveller," by Clinton Dangerfield, from *Lippincott's Magazine*.

Messrs. Longmans, Green & Co. for " Pen and Ink," by Andrew Lang.

Messrs. Robert M. McBride & Co. for " West India Dock Road," from *London Lamps,* by Thomas Burke.

Mr. Erskine MacDonald, London, for " The Airman's Battle Hymn," from *The Red, Red Dawn,* by James A. Mackreth; " Drinking Song," from *Folly,* by Theodore Maynard.

Mr. John S. McGroarty, Los Angeles, for " The Port o' Heart's Desire," by John S. McGroarty.

The Macmillan Company for " The Bronco that would not be broken of Dancing," from *The Chinese Nightingale, and Other Poems,* by Vachel Lindsay; " Sea Fever " and " To his Mother," from *The Story of a Round-House, and Other Poems,* by John Masefield; " Battle Cry " and " Let me live out my Years," from *The Quest,* by John G. Neihardt.

Messrs. Macmillan & Co., London, for " In Defence of the Bush," from *The Man from Snowy River,* by A. B. Paterson.

Mr. Elkin Mathews, London, for " Hastings Mill," from *Sailor Town and Sea Songs,* and " Shipmates," from *Songs in Sail,* by Cicely Fox-Smith.

Mr. Thomas Bird Mosher for " A Litany," from *Amphora,* by Gertrude M. Hort.

Mr. Le Roy Phillips for " Boot Hill," from *Cactus and Pine,* by Sharlot M. Hall.

Messrs. G. P. Putnam's Sons for " The Jackpot," from *Rhymes of Ironquill,* by Eugene F. Ware.

Mr. Grant Richards, London, for " The Last Journey" (" Epilogue "), from *The Testament of John*

Davidson, by John Davidson; " West India Dock Road," from *London Lamps,* by Thomas Burke.

Messrs. Charles Scribner's Sons for " I have a Rendezvous with Death," from *Poems,* by Alan Seeger; " Requiem," from *Poems and Ballads,* by Robert Louis Stevenson.

Mr. Martin Secker, London, and Mr. J. H. Flecker for " To a Poet a Thousand Years Hence," from *Poems,* by James Elroy Flecker.

Messrs. Small, Maynard & Co. for " Spring Song," by Bliss Carman, from *Songs from Vagabondia,* by Bliss Carman and Richard Hovey; " Sleepin' Out " and " Trail's End," from *Cowboy Lyrics,* by Robert V. Carr; " The Sea Gipsy," by Richard Hovey, from *Songs from Vagabondia.*

Mr. T. Fisher Unwin, London, and the *New York American* for " The Hell-Gate of Soissons," from *Hell-Gate of Soissons,* by Herbert Kaufman.

Messrs. M. Witmark & Sons for " Walk, Damn You, Walk," from *Jim Marshall's New Pianner, and Other Western Stories,* by William De Vere.

Yale University Press and *Poetry* for " The Horse Thief," from *The Burglar of the Zodiac,* by William Rose Benét.

The *Century Magazine* for " Fame is a Food that Dead Men Eat," by Austin Dobson.

Contemporary Verse for " Courage, mon Ami!" by Willard Wattles.

Land and Water, London, for " R.N.V.R.," by N. M. F. Corbett.

McClure's Magazine for " Deserted Roads," by Berton Braley.

The Masses for " Highways," by Leslie Nelson Jennings.

The *New Witness,* London, for " Gratias Ago," by Geoffrey Howard.

The *New York Evening Sun* for " Portrait of an Old Sea Captain," by Dana Burnet; " A Gentleman of Fifty Soliloquizes," by Don Marquis.

The *New York Times* for " Song of Brother Hilario," by Stephen Chalmers; "The Last Trail," by J. Corson Miller; "Roosevelt — the Leader," by Mary Siegrist.

The *New York Tribune* for " The Boys who Never Grew Up," by Charles Law Watkins.

The *Outing Magazine* for " The End of the Season," by W. G. Tinckom-Fernandez.

Reedy's Mirror for " His Share," by Kendall Harrison.

The *Saturday Evening Post* for " The New Route," by Berton Braley; " The Best Road of All," by Charles Hanson Towne.

Scribner's Magazine for " A Vagrant's Epitaph," by Theodore Roberts.

The Smart Set for " The Broke Brigade," by Frank Lillie Pollock.

The Spectator, London, for "Hamish," by C. Hilton Brown; " Lazarus," by Alfred Cochrane.

Town Topics for " Bohemia."

CONTENTS

SONGS OF MEN

THE VOORTREKKER

*The gull shall whistle in his wake, the blind wave break
    in fire.*
He shall fulfil God's utmost will, unknowing His desire.
And he shall see old planets change and alien stars arise,
And give the gale his seaworn sail in shadow of new skies.
*Strong lust of gear shall drive him forth and hunger arm
    his hand,*
*To wring his food from the desert rude, his pittance from
    the sand.*
*His neighbours' smoke shall vex his eyes, their voices
    break his rest.*
*He shall go forth till south is north, sullen and dispos-
    sessed.*
He shall desire loneliness and his desire shall bring,
*Hard on his heels, a thousand wheels, a People and a
    King.*
*He shall come back on his own track, and by his scarce-
    cooled camp*
*There shall he meet the roaring street, the derrick and
    the stamp:*
*There he shall blaze a nation's ways with hatchet and
    with brand,*
Till on his last-won wilderness an Empire's outposts stand.

SONGS OF MEN

OUT THERE SOMEWHERE

As I was hiking past the woods, the cool and sleepy
    summer woods,
  I saw a guy a-talking to the sunshine in the air;
Thinks I, he 's going to have a fit — I 'll stick
    around and watch a bit;
  But he paid no attention, hardly knowing I was
    there.

He must have been a college guy, for he was talking
    big and high, —
  The trees were standing all around as silent as a
    church —
A little closer I saw he was manufacturing poetry,
  Just like a Mocker sitting on a pussy-willow perch.

I squatted down and rolled a smoke and listened
    to each word he spoke;
  He never stumbled, reared or broke; he never
    missed a word,
And though he was a Bo like me, he 'd been a gent
    once, I could see;
  I ain't much strong on poetry, but this is what I
    heard:

" We 'll dance a merry saraband from here to
    drowsy Samarcand;
  Along the sea, across the land, the birds are fly-
    ing South,

And you, my sweet Penelope, out there somewhere
      you wait for me,
  With buds of roses in your hair and kisses on
     your mouth.

" The mountains are all hid in mist; the valley is
      like amethyst;
  The poplar leaves they turn and twist; oh, silver,
     silver green!
Out there somewhere along the sea a ship is wait-
      ing patiently,
  While up the beach the bubbles slip with white
     afloat between.

" The tide-hounds race far up the shore — the hunt
      is on! The breakers roar,
  (Her spars are tipped with gold and o'er her deck
     the spray is flung);
The buoys that rollick in the bay, they nod the way,
     they nod the way!
  The hunt is up! I am the prey! The hunter's
     bow is strung! "

" Out there somewhere," — says I to me — " By
      Gosh! I guess that 's poetry!
  Out there somewhere — Penelope, with kisses
     on her mouth!"
And then, thinks I, " O college guy, your talk it
      gets me in the eye,
  The North *is* creeping in the air; the birds *are*
     flying South,"

And yet, the sun was shining down, a-blazing on
    the little town,
  A mile or so 'way down the track a-dancing in
    the sun.
But somehow, as I waited there, there came a
    shiver in the air;
  " The birds are flying South," says he — " The
    winter has begun."

Says I, " Then let 's be on the float; you certainly
    have got my goat;
  You make me hungry in my throat for seeing
    things that 's new.
Out there somewhere we 'll ride the range a-looking
    for the new and strange;
  My feet are tired and need a change. Come on!
    It 's up to you!"

" There ain't no sweet Penelope somewhere that 's
    longing much for me,
  But I can smell the blundering sea and hear the
    rigging hum;
And I can hear the whispering lips that fly before
    the outbound ships,
  And I can hear the breakers on the sand
    a-booming, ' Come! ' "

And then that slim, poetic guy, he turned and looked
    me in the eye :
  " . . . It 's overland and overland and overseas
    to — where? "

" Most anywhere that is n't here," I says. His face
     went kind of queer:
  " The place we 're in is always *here*. The other
     place is *there*."

He smiled, though, as my eye caught his. " Then
     what a lot of *there* there is
  To go and see and go and see and go and see
     some more."
He did a fancy step or two. Says he, " I think I 'll
     go with you — "
  . . . Two moons, and we were baking in the
     straits at Singapore.

Around the world and back again; we saw it all,
     The mist and rain
  In England and the dry old plain from Needles
     to Berdoo.
We kept a-rambling all the time. I rustled grub,
     he rustled rhyme —
  Blind-baggage, hoof it, ride or climb — we always
     put it through.

Just for a con I 'd like to know (yes, he crossed
     over long ago;
  And he was *right*, believe me, Bo!) if some-
     where in the South,
Down where the clouds lie on the sea, he found his
     sweet Penelope,
  With buds of roses in her hair and kisses on her
     mouth.

THE BELOVED VAGABOND

You who were once so careless, I can recall you
    now,
Your blue-gray visionary eyes, your great and
    open brow,
With naught to bind your heart-strings, and all
    the world in fee,
You went where all the roads lead, beyond the
    farthest sea.

Lover of space and skyline, what vision seared your
    eyes?
What gypsy word was winged to you that bade you
    gird and rise?
What thread of smoke sent onward your restless,
    eager feet?
What vagrant heart was waiting your wayward
    heart to greet?

We, who are kin to the city, across the candles
    praise
Your tales of camps in twilight, your great and
    gallant ways,
Your knowledge of the mysteries deep-hidden by
    the wood,
The pagan trust you placed in man, the world you
    found so good.

Then leave a *patrin* for mine eyes that I may follow
    too,
Some day when all the world grows dim, and I
    shall beckon you;

Across the distant moorland, from beacon furze
    piled high,
May I, the newest rover, see your fire against the
    sky!

PEN AND INK

Ye wanderers that were my sires,
    Who read men's fortunes in the hand,
Who voyaged with your smithy fires
    From waste to waste across the land,
Why did you leave for garth and town
    Your life by heath and river's brink?
Why lay your gipsy freedom down
    And doom your child to Pen and Ink?

You wearied of your wild-wood meal
    That crowned, or failed to crown, the day,
Too honest or too tame to steal,
    You broke into the beaten way:
Plied loom or awl like other men
    And learned to love the guineas' clink —
Oh, recreant sires, who doomed me then
    To earn so few — with Pen and Ink!

Where it hath fallen the tree must lie.
    'T is over-late for *me* to roam,
Yet the caged bird who hears the cry
    Of his wild fellows fleeting home,
May feel no sharper pang than mine,
    Who seem to hear, whene'er I think,
Spate in the stream, and wind in pine,
    Call me to quit dull Pen and Ink.

For then the spirit wandering,
  That sleeps within the blood, awakes;
For then the summer and the spring
  I fain would meet by streams and lakes,
But ah, my birthright long is sold,
  For custom chains me, link on link,
And I must get me, as of old,
  Back to my tools, to Pen and Ink.

HIGHWAYS

Who 's learned the lure of trodden ways,
  And walked them up and down,
May love a steeple in a mist,
  But cannot love a town.

Who 's worn a bit of purple once
  Can never, never lie
All smothered in a little box
  When stars are in the sky.

Who 's sipped old port in Venice glass
  May thirst for better brew —
He 's drunk an amber wine of sun
  And wet his mouth with dew!

Who 's ground the grist of trodden ways —
  The gray dust and the brown —
May love red tiling two miles off —
  But cannot love a town.

THE TRAVELLER

Child of the shifting desert sands,
Strange ways he oft had trod;
And he had known the loneliest lands,
Shaped by the hand of God.

But not until the city's ways
Flowed past his mute distress
Learned he in bitterness of heart
The depths of loneliness.

THE BROKE BRIGADE

When the last string snaps and a man goes broke,
　He turns to the woods or the sea;
He cuts clean loose from the home-bred folk,
　While love and honor go up like smoke,
And life is a gamble and death is a joke,
　And the universe good to see.

There 's a brand-new sort of a fate for him;
They may languish early and late for him,
The bird on the wing is a mate for him,
　And the hawk on the hunt goes free.

There 's the brown and the gloom of the forest
　　track
　Where the deer go ghostly by;
There 's the starving camp and the deadweight
　　pack,
　The moose-hide lodge or the trapper's shack
And a wolf's fierce life in the pine woods black
　And the freedom of the sky.

There 's the plunging deck and the jarring screw,
  And the oilskins bright with foam,
The stokehole's blaze and its naked crew,
  Or the topsails drenched with the Gulf Stream
    dew,
And the sharp, salt breath of the landless blue,
  When a man forgets his home.

We know it, my friends of the " broke brigade,"
  Pals of the plain and sea;
Single-handed and unafraid,
  The artists of life and the fools of trade,
But we think we know how the game is played,
  And we know where it 's best to be.

There are some that may wait and pray for us;
There is luck that never will stay for us;
But the woods and the waves will make way for us,
  When the " broke brigade " goes free!

A LITANY

Come thou at morn before I fight,
To cast a glamour on my sight,
Until I think the odds but light
    Though men with gods must cope!
But when I wait at set of sun
The news that tarries — " Lost or Won ? "—
By all the pangs I did not shun,
    Deliver me from hope!

If fealty with my tribe I break,
Their scourge let me unshrinking take,

And from the cup they give me, make
    Libation to their law!
But when they say my outworn lust
Must wed my forehead to the dust
Or bar my soul from further trust,
    Deliver me from awe!

If vice has marred my neighbor's fate,
May I deride his word " too late! "
And — to my last sheaf! — re-create
    His locust-eaten years!
But when vice, wild with sudden loss,
Its alms in every lap would toss,
Or clamour, dying, from its cross,
    Deliver me from tears!

If chance should to my workshop send
A certain, silent, fleshless friend,
Thou, while day lasts, Thy legions lend,
    And hold him from the stair!
But when the best tool slips away,
And he must idle who would stay —
If once against the Dark I 'd pray,
    Deliver me from prayer!

LET ME LIVE OUT MY YEARS

Let me live out my years in heat of blood!
    Let me die drunken with the dreamer's wine!
Let me not see this soul-house built of mud
    Go toppling to the dust — a vacant shrine!

Let me go quickly like a candle-light
    Snuffed out just at the heyday of its glow!

Give me high noon — and let it then be night!
  Thus would I go.

And grant me when I face the grisly Thing,
  One haughty cry to pierce the gray Perhaps!
Let me be as a tune-swept fiddle-string
  That feels the Master Melody — and snaps!

THE GREEN INN

I sicken of men's company,
  The crowded tavern's din,
Where all day long with oath and song
  Sit they who entrance win,
So come I out from noise and rout
  To rest in God's Green Inn.

Here none may mock an empty purse
  Or ragged coat and poor,
But Silence waits within the gates,
  And Peace beside the door;
The weary guest is welcomest,
  The richest pays no score.

The roof is high and arched and blue,
  The floor is spread with pine;
On my four walls the sunlight falls
  In golden flecks and fine;
And swift and fleet on noiseless feet
  The Four Winds bring me wine.

Upon my board they set their store —
  Great drinks mixed cunningly,

Wherein the scent of furze is blent
   With odor of the sea;
As from a cup I drink it up
   To thrill the veins of me.

It 's I will sit in God's Green Inn
   Unvexed by man or ghost,
Yet ever fed and comforted,
   Companioned by mine host,
And watched at night by that white light
   High swung from coast to coast.

Oh, you who in the House of Strife
   Quarrel and game and sin,
Come out and see what cheer may be
   For starveling souls and thin
Who come at last from drought and fast
   To sit in God's Green Inn.

"HE DOES NOT DIE"

He does not die who can bequeath
   Some influence to the land he knows,
Or dares, persistent, interwreath
   Love permanent with the wild hedgerows;
     He does not die but still remains
     Substantiate with his darling plains.

The spring's superb adventure calls
   His dust athwart the woods to flame;
His boundary-river's secret falls
   Perpetuate and repeat his name.
     He rides his loud October sky;
     He does not die. He does not die.

The beeches know the accustomed head
  Which loved them; and a peopled air
Beneath their benediction spread
  Comforts the silence everywhere;
    For native ghosts return and these
    Perfect the mystery of the trees.

So, therefore, though myself be crosst
  The shuddering of that dreadful day
When friend and fire and home are lost
  And even children drawn away —
    The passer-by shall hear me still,
    A boy that sings on Duncton Hill.

THE JACKPOT

I sauntered down through Europe,
  I wandered up the Nile,
I sought the mausoleums where the mummied
    Pharaohs lay;
I found the sculptured tunnel
  Where quietly in style
Imperial sarcophagi concealed the royal clay.
  Above the vault was graven deep the motto of
    the crown:
  " Who openeth a jackpot may not always rake
    it down."

It 's strange what deep impressions
  Are made by little things.
Within the granite tunneling I saw a dingy cleft;
It was a cryptic chamber:
  I drew and got four kings,

But on a brief comparison I laid them down and
    left,
  Because upon the granite stood that sentence
    bold and brown:
  " Who openeth a jackpot may not always rake
    it down."

I make this observation;
    A man with such a hand
Has psychologic feelings which perhaps he should
    not feel,
But I was somewhat rattled
    And in a foreign land,
And had some dim suspicions as I had not watched
    the deal.
  And there was that inscription, too, in words
    that seemed to frown:
  " Who openeth a jackpot may not always rake
    it down."

These letters were not graven
    In Anglo-Saxon tongue;
Perhaps if you had seen them you had idly passed
    them by;
I studied erudition
    When I was somewhat young;
I recognized the language when it struck my clas-
    sic eye;
  I saw a maxim suitable for monarch or for
    clown:
  " Who openeth a jackpot may not always rake
    it down."

Detesting metaphysics,
    I cannot help but put
A philosophic moral where I think it ought to
    hang;
I 've seen a boom for office
    Grow feeble at the root,
Then change into a boomlet — then to a boom-
    erang.
    In caucus or convention, in village or in town:
    " Who openeth a jackpot may not always rake
    it down."

THE SINGER'S QUEST

I 've been wandering, listening for a song,
Dreaming of a melody, all my life long . . .
The lilting tune that God sang to rock the tides
    asleep,
And crooned above the cradled stars before they
    learned to creep.

O, there was laughter in it and many a merry
    chime,
Before He had turned moralist, grown old before
    His time,
And He was happy, trolling out His great blithe-
    hearted tune,
Before He slung the little earth beneath the sun
    and moon.

But I know that somewhere that song is rolling on,
Like flutes along the midnight, like trumpets in
    the dawn;

It throbs across the sunset and stirs the poplar tree
And rumbles in the long low thunder of the sea.
. . . .

First-love sang me one note and heart-break
taught me two,
A child has told me three notes, and soon I 'll
know it through;
And when I stand before the Throne I 'll hum it
low and sly,
Watching for a great light of welcome in His eye, . . .

" Put a white raiment on him and a harp into his
hand,
And golden sandals on his feet and tell the saints
to stand
A little farther off unless they wish to hear the
truth,
For this blessed lucky sinner is going to sing about
my youth! "

SPRING SONG

Make me over, mother April,
When the sap begins to stir!
When thy flowery hand delivers
All the mountain-prisoned rivers,
And thy great heart beats and quivers
To revive the days that were,
Make me over, mother April,
When the sap begins to stir!

Take my dust and all my dreaming,
Count my heart-beats one by one,

Send them where the winters perish;
Then some golden noon recherish
And restore them in the sun,
Flower and scent and dust and dreaming,
With their heart-beats every one!

Set me in the urge and tide-drift
Of the streaming hosts a-wing!
Breast of scarlet, throat of yellow,
Raucous challenge, wooings mellow —
Every migrant is my fellow,
Making northward with the spring.
Loose me in the urge and tide-drift
Of the streaming hosts a-wing!

Shrilling pipe or fluting whistle,
In the valleys come again;
Fife of frog and call of tree-toad,
All my brothers, five or three-toed,
With their revel no more vetoed,
Making music in the rain;
Shrilling pipe or fluting whistle,
In the valleys come again.

Make me of thy seed to-morrow,
When the sap begins to stir!
Tawny light-foot, sleepy bruin,
Bright-eyes in the orchard ruin,
Gnarl the good life goes askew in,
Whiskey-jack, or tanager, —
Make me anything to-morrow,
When the sap begins to stir!

Make me even (how do I know?)
Like my friend the gargoyle there;
It may be the heart within him
Swells that doltish hands should pin him
Fixed forever in mid-air.
Make me even sport for swallows,
Like the soaring gargoyle there!

Give me the old clue to follow,
Through the labyrinth of night!
Clod of clay with heart of fire,
Things that burrow and aspire,
With the vanishing desire,
For the perishing delight, —
Only the old clue to follow,
Through the labyrinth of night!

Make me over, mother April,
When the sap begins to stir!
Fashion me from swamp or meadow,
Garden plot or ferny shadow,
Hyacinth or humble burr!
Make me over, mother April,
When the sap begins to stir!

Let me hear the far, low summons,
When the silver winds return;
Rills that run and streams that stammer,
Goldenwing with his loud hammer,
Icy brooks that brawl and clamor,
Where the Indian willows burn;
Let me hearken to the calling,
When the silver winds return,

Till recurring and recurring,
Long since wandered and come back,
Like a whim of Grieg's or Gounod's,
This same self, bird, bud, or Bluenose,
Some day I may capture (who knows?)
Just the one last joy I lack,
Waking to the far new summons,
When the old spring winds come back.

For I have no choice of being,
When the sap begins to climb, —
Strong insistence, sweet intrusion,
Vasts and verges of illusion, —
So I win, to time's confusion,
The one perfect pearl of time,
Joy and joy and joy forever,
Till the sap forgets to climb!

Make me over in the morning
From the rag-bag of the world!
Scraps of dream and duds of daring,
Home-brought stuff from far sea-faring,
Faded colors once so flaring,
Shreds of banners long since furled!
Hues of ash and glints of glory,
In the rag-bag of the world!

Let me taste the old immortal
Indolence of life once more;
Not recalling nor foreseeing,
Let the great slow joys of being
Well my heart through as of yore!
Let me taste the old immortal
Indolence of life once more!

Give me the old drink for rapture,
The delirium to drain,
All my fellows drank in plenty
At the Three Score Inns and Twenty
From the mountains to the main!
Give me the old drink for rapture,
The delirium to drain!

Only make me over, April,
When the sap begins to stir!
Make me man or make me woman,
Make me oaf or ape or human,
Cup of flower or cone of fir;
Make me anything but neuter
When the sap begins to stir!

"WHENCE COMETH MY HELP"

Let me sleep among the shadows of the mountains
        when I die,
    In the murmur of the pines and sliding streams,
Where the long day loiters by
Like a cloud across the sky
        And the moon-drenched night is musical with
        dreams.

Lay me down within a canyon of the mountains,
        far away,
    In a valley filled with dim and rosy light,
Where the flashing rivers play
Out across the golden day
        And a noise of many waters brims the night.

Let me lie where glinting rivers ramble down the
    slanted glade
    Under bending alders garrulous and cool,
Where they gather in the shade
To the dazzling, sheer cascade,
    Where they plunge and sleep within the peb-
    bled pool.

All the wisdom, all the beauty, I have lived for un-
    aware
    Came upon me by the rote of highland rills;
I have seen God walking there
In the solemn soundless air
    When the morning wakened wonder in the hills.

I am what the mountains made me of their green
    and gold and gray,
    Of the dawnlight and the moonlight and the
    foam.
Mighty mothers far away,
Ye who washed my soul in spray,
    I am coming, mother mountains, coming home.

When I draw my dreams about me, when I leave
    the darkling plain
    Where my soul forgets to soar and learns to
    plod,
I shall go back home again
To the kingdoms of the rain,
    To the blue purlieus of Heaven, nearer God.

Where the rose of dawn blooms earlier across the
    miles of mist,
    Between the tides of sundown and moonrise,

I shall keep a lover's tryst
With the gold and amethyst,
    With the stars for my companions in the skies.

" HE DONE HIS DAMDEST "

I ask that when my spirit quits this shell of mortal
    clay
And o'er the trail across the range pursues its
    silent way,
That no imposing marble shaft may mark the spot
    where rest
The tailings of the bard who sang the praises of the
    West.
But, that above them may be placed a slab of white
    or gray,
And on it but the epitaph carved in the earlier day,
Upon the headboard of a man who did the best he
    could
To have the bad deeds of his life o'ershadowed by
    the good:
    " He Done His Damdest."

Engrave upon the polished face of that plain, sim-
    ple stone,
No nicely worded sentiment intended to condone
The sins of an eventful life, nor say the virtues
    wiped
Away the stains of vice — in lines original or
    swiped;
That rough but honest sentiment that stood above
    the head
Of one who wore his boots into his final earthly bed

Is good enough for me to have above my mould'ring
    clay —
Just give the name and day I quit and underneath
    it say:
      "He Done His Damdest."

Some who are overstocked with phony piety may
    raise
Their hands in blank amazement at the sentiment
    and gaze
Upon the simple marble slab 'neath which the
    sleeper lies,
With six or seven different kinds of horror in their
    eyes;
But hardy sons and daughters of this brave and
    rugged West
Will see a tribute in the line so pointedly ex-
    pressed —
And what more earnest tribute could be paid to
    any man
Whose weary feet have hit the trail towards the
    Mystery, than:
      "He Done His Damdest."

THE BEST ROAD OF ALL

I like a road that leads away to prospects white
    and fair,
A road that is an ordered road, like a nun's evening
    prayer;
But best of all I love a road that leads to God
    knows where.

You come upon it suddenly — you cannot seek it
 out;
It's like a secret still unheard and never noised
 about;
But when you see it, gone at once is every lurking
 doubt.

It winds beside some rushing stream where aspens
 lightly quiver;
It follows many a broken field by many a shining
 river;
It seems to lead you on and on, forever and forever!

You tramp along its dusty way beneath the shad-
 owy trees,
And hear beside you chattering birds or happy
 booming bees,
And all around you golden sounds, the green
 leaves' litanies.

And here's a hedge and there's a cot; and then,
 strange, sudden turns —
A dip, a rise, a little glimpse where the red sunset
 burns;
A bit of sky at evening time, the scent of hidden
 ferns.

A winding road, a loitering road, the finger mark
 of God,
Traced when the Maker of the world leaned over
 ways untrod.
See! Here He smiled His glowing smile, and lo,
 the golden-rod!

I like a road that wanders straight; the King's
    highway is fair,
And lovely are the sheltered lanes that take you
    here and there;
But best of all I love a road that leads to God
    knows where.

AN ISLAND SONG

O the grey rocks of the islands and the hemlock
    green above them,
The foam beneath the wild-rose bloom, the star
    above the shoal.
When I 'm old and weary I 'll wake my heart to
    love them,
For the blue ways of the islands are wound about
    my soul.

Here in the early even when the young, grey dew is
    falling,
And the king-heron seeks his mate beyond the lone-
    liest wild,
Still your heart in the twilight, and you 'll hear the
    river calling
Through all her outmost islands to seek her last-
    born child.

A VAGRANT'S EPITAPH

Change was his mistress, Chance his counselor.
Love could not keep him, Duty forged no chain.
The wide seas and the mountains called to him,
And gray dawns saw his campfires in the rain.

Sweet hands might tremble! Ay, but he must go.
Revel might hold him for a little space,
But, turning past the laughter and the lamps,
His eyes must ever catch the luring face.

Dear eyes might question! Yea, and melt
     again!
Rare lips, a-quiver, silently implore;
But ever must he turn his furtive head
And hear the other summons at the door.

Change was his mistress, Chance his counselor.
The dark pines knew his whistle up the trail.
Why tarries he to-day? And yesternight
Adventure lit her stars without avail!

"GRATIAS AGO"

Since of earth, air and water,
The gods have made me part —
Let every human sin be mine
Except the thankless heart!
Privileged greatly, I partake
Of sleep and death and birth;
And kneeling, drink the sacrament —
The good red wine of earth.

I shall not ask the High Gods
For aught that they can give;
They gave the greatest gift of all
When first they bade me live.
Great gift of dawn and starlight,
Of sea and grass and river;

With leave to toil and laugh and weep
And praise the Sun forever!

Be death the end or not the end,
Too richly blest am I
To seek the hill behind the hill,
The sky behind the sky.
Let the red earth that bore me
Give me her call again,
And I'll lie still beneath her flowers
And sleep and not complain.

Let those the gods have blinded
Hold their long feud with Fate —
And clutch at toys that never yet
Could make one mean man great.
Let those that Earth has bastarded
Fret and contrive and plan —
But I will enter like an heir
The old estate of man!

TO A POET A THOUSAND YEARS HENCE

I who am dead a thousand years,
    And wrote this sweet archaic song,
Send you my words for messengers
    The way I shall not pass along.

I care not if you bridge the seas,
    Or ride secure the cruel sky,
Or build consummate palaces
    Of metal or of masonry.

But have you wine and music still,
   And statues and a bright-eyed love,
And foolish thoughts of good and ill,
   And prayers to them who sit above?

How shall we conquer? Like a wind
   That falls at eve our fancies blow,
And old Mæonides the blind
   Said it three thousand years ago.

Oh, friend unseen, unborn, unknown,
   Student of our sweet English tongue,
Read out my words at night alone:
   I was a poet, I was young.

Since I can never see your face,
   And never shake you by the hand,
I send my soul through time and space
   To greet you. You will understand.

A GENTLEMAN OF FIFTY SOLILOQUIZES

Some ten or twelve old friends of yours and mine,
   If we spoke truly, are not friends at all.
They never were. That accident divine,
   A friendship, not so often may befall!

But as the dull years pass with dragging feet,
   Within them waxes, in us wanes, esteem;
For weakly, and half conscious of deceit,
   We gave them cause an equal love to dream.

Could we have told some fool with haggard face
  Who bared his soul, so sure we'd understand,
His little tragedy was commonplace? . . .
  We lied. We stretched to him a brother's hand.

He loved us for it, and mere ruth has kept
Our jaws from yawning while he drooled and
    wept.

The valor cold to be ourselves we lack;
  And so from strands of kindness misconstrued
And lenient moments, careless threads and slack,
  We're meshed within a web of habitude.

And often these are worthier men than we;
  But that itself, in time, becomes offense;
We're burdened with this damned nobility
  That's forced upon us, which we must recom-
    pense.

We loathe ourselves for being insincere,
  And lavish generous deeds to hide the fact:
For who would wound these hearts? Thus we ap-
    pear
  Thrice loyal friends in word and look and act!

And golden lies with which we save them pain
But serve to make their true regard more fain.

Should chance strike out of me some human heat—
  Leap not at that and think to grasp my soul!
I flee new bonds. Myself must still retreat
  Down devious ways to keep me free and whole.

Give me your mind, and I will give you mine;
  Then should it change, no heart will bleed or
    burn.
Give me your wits. I want no heart of thine —
  You 'll ask too much of life-blood in return.

There was a golden lad in years long gone . . .
  We twain together left the ways of men
And roamed the starry heights, the fields of dawn,
  In youth and gladness. This comes not again.

Give me your mirth. It bores me when you weep.
My loves you cannot touch. They 're buried deep.

THE ROAD TO VAGABONDIA

He was sitting on a doorstep as I went strolling
    by;
A lonely little beggar with a wistful, homesick eye —
And he was n't what you 'd borrow
And he was n't what you 'd steal —
But I guessed his heart was breaking,
So I whistled him to heel.

They had stoned him through the city streets and
      naught the city cared,
But I was heading outward and the roads are
      sweeter shared,
So I took him for a comrade and I whistled him
      away —
On the road to Vagabondia that lies across the day.

Yellow dog he was; but bless you — he was just
    the chap for me!
For I 'd rather have an inch of dog than miles of
    pedigree.
So we stole away together on the road that has no
    end
With a new-coined day to fling away and all the
    stars to spend!

Oh, to walk the road at morning, when the wind is
    blowing clean,
And the yellow daisies fling their gold across a
    world of green —
For the wind it heals the heart-aches and the sun
    it dries the scars,
On the road to Vagabondia that lies beneath the
    stars.

'T was the wonder of the going cast a spell about
    our feet —
We walked because the world was young, because
    the way was sweet;
And we slept in wild-rose meadows by the little
    wayside farms,
'Til the Dawn came up the highroad with the dead
    moon in her arms.

Oh, the Dawn it went before us through a shining
    lane of skies,
And the Dream was at our heartstrings and the
    light was in our eyes,

And we made no boast of glory and we made no
　　boast of birth,
On the road to Vagabondia that lies across the
　　earth.

THE END OF THE SEASON

There 's a keen wind searching the marshes
　　With a tang of the open sea,
And a wind-blown sky of opal
　　For a sense of Infinity —
As a dog and I, together,
Sit close and curse the weather
And wait for the grey-goose feather,
　　While a cramp strikes to the knee.

There 's the loneliness of Sahara
　　Except for his patient head,
And his wet nose lifted to windward
　　For a squadron fan-wise spread —
As we sigh that the summer 's over,
With our long tramps through the clover,
I and this old land rover,
　　Though scarce a word is said.

There 's a stealthy sea-fog stalking
　　Across the ghostly dune,
As we turn us empty-handed
　　With a half-forgotten tune —
Some day we 'll quit our roaming:
Together in the gloaming,
Twin shades that would be homing
　　Beneath a hunting moon.

ROOFS

The road is wide and the stars are out and the
    breath of night is sweet,
And this is the time when wanderlust should seize
    upon my feet,
But I'm glad to turn from the open road and the
    starlight on my face,
And leave the splendor of out-of-doors for a hu-
    man dwelling place.

I never have known a vagabond who really liked
    to roam,
All up and down the streets of the world and never
    have a home.
The tramp who slept in your barn last night and
    left at the break of day
Will wander on until he finds another place to stay.

The Gipsy man sleeps in his cart with canvas over-
    head,
Or else he crawls into a tent when it is time for
    bed.
He will take his ease upon the grass as long as the
    sun is high
But when it is dark he wants a roof to keep away
    the sky.

If you call the Gipsy a vagabond I think you do him
    wrong,
For he never goes a-traveling but he takes his
    home along.

And the only reason a road is good, as every wan-
derer knows,
Is just because of the homes, the homes, the homes
to which it goes.

They say life is a highway and its milestones are
the years,
And now and then there's a toll-gate where you
pay your way with tears.
It's a rough road and a steep road and it stretches
broad and far,
But it leads at last to a Golden Town where Gol-
den Houses are.

BOHEMIA

Bohemia! Bohemia! The land of art and song,
The land of genius far removed from Mammon's
greedy throng;
Whose glories glad the author's pen, whose joy the
poet sings,
The kingdom unconventional, the realm of *different*
things.
The empire reached by weary climbs of many a
dingy stair,
The home of shining velvet coats and weird and
wondrous hair;
Where grand and gorgeous ties are worn to hide a
threadbare shirt,
And inspiration soars and sings 'mid Chinese gods
and dirt.

Bohemia! Bohemia! Where hearts are open wide,
And each one's purse his neighbor's is, with
naught, alas, inside!

Where sparks of genius bravely strive to light the
    attic rooms,
And budding talent does its best but ah! so seldom
    blooms.
Where coffee 's always brown and thick and wine
    is blue and thin,
And every doorway has its wolf who strives to enter in;
Where " feasts of fancy " form too oft the toiler's
    daily fare,
And unpaid bills are plentiful as dollar bills are rare.

Bohemia! Bohemia! The world of hopes and fears,
Of themes and dreams and cigarettes, free lunches,
    beers and tears,
Impressions, color-schemes and dust, starvation
    smoke and debts,
Despair and work and dunning notes and " edi-
    tor's regrets."
Forgive me if I do not say I love thee, but I find
They praise thee most who 've won success and
    left thy courts behind;
And if perchance the day should come when from
    thy clutches free,
I live once more as white man should, I 'll sing in
    praise of thee.

COURAGE, MON AMI!

Oh, it is good to camp with the spirit,
Oh, it is jaunty to walk with the mind,
When the soul sees all the future to share it
Knowing the road that stretches behind.

Courage, my comrade, the devil is dying!
Here's the bright sun and a cloud scudding free;
The touch of your hand is too near for denying,
And laughter's a tavern sufficient for me.

Hang your old hat on the smoke-mellowed rafter,
Strike an old song on your crazy guitar;
Hey, hustle, old lady, it's heaven we're after —
God, but I'm glad we can be what we are!

EVOLUTION

When you were a Tadpole and I was a Fish,
In the Paleozoic time,
And side by side on the ebbing tide
We sprawled through the ooze and slime,
Or skittered with many a caudal flip
Through the depths of the Cambrian fen —
My heart was rife with the joy of life
For I loved you even then.

Mindless we lived, mindless we loved,
And mindless at last we died;
And deep in the rift of a Caradoc drift
We slumbered side by side.
The world turned on in the lathe of time,
The hot sands heaved amain,
Till we caught our breath from the womb of death
And crept into life again.

We were Amphibians, scaled and tailed,
And drab as a dead man's hand.
We coiled at ease 'neath the dripping trees
Or trailed through the mud and sand,

Croaking and blind, with our three-clawed feet,
Writing a language dumb,
With never a spark in the empty dark
To hint at a life to come.

And happy we loved, happy we lived,
And happy we died once more.
And our forms were rolled in the clinging mold
Of a Neocomian shore.
The æons came and the æons fled,
And the sleep that wrapped us fast
Was riven away in a newer day,
And the night of death was past.

Then light and swift through the jungle trees
We swung in our airy flights,
Or breathed in the balms of the fronded palms
In the hush of the moonless nights.
And oh, what beautiful years were these
When our hearts clung each to each;
When life was filled and our senses thrilled
In the first faint dawn of speech!

Thus life by life and love by love
We passed through the cycles strange,
And breath by breath and death by death
We followed the chain of change.
Till there came a time in the law of life
When over the nursing sod
The shadows broke and the soul awoke
In a strange, dim dream of God.

I was thewed like an Aurochs bull
And tusked like the great Cave-Bear,

And you, my sweet, from head to feet,
Were gowned in your glorious hair.
Deep in the gloom of a fireless cave,
When the night fell o'er the plain,
And the moon hung red o'er the river bed,
We mumbled the bones of the slain.

I flaked a flint to a cutting edge,
And shaped it with brutish craft;
I broke a shank from the woodland dank,
And fitted it, head and haft.
Then I hid me close to the reedy tarn,
Where the Mammoth came to drink —
Through brawn and bone I drave the stone,
And slew him upon the brink.

Loud I howled through the moonlit wastes,
Loud answered our kith and kin;
From west and east to the crimson feast
The clan came trooping in.
O'er joint and gristle and padded hoof,
We fought and clawed and tore,
And cheek by jowl, with many a growl,
We talked the marvel o'er.

I carved that fight on a reindeer bone
With rude and hairy hand;
I pictured his fall on the cavern wall
That men might understand.
For we lived by blood and the right of might,
Ere human laws were drawn,
And the age of sin did not begin
Till our brutal tusks were gone.

And that was a million years ago,
In a time that no man knows;
Yet here to-night in the mellow light
We sit at Delmonico's.
Your eyes are deep as the Devon springs,
Your hair is as dark as jet,
Your years are few, your life is new,
Your soul untried, and yet —

Our trail is on the Kimmeridge clay,
And the scarp of the Purbeck flags;
We have left our bones in the Bagshot stones,
And deep in the Coralline crags.
Our love is old, our lives are old,
And death shall come amain.
Should it come to-day, what man may say
We shall not live again?

God wrought our souls from the Tremadoc beds
And furnished them wings to fly;
He sowed our spawn in the world's dim dawn,
And I know that it shall not die —
Though cities have sprung above the graves
Where the crook-boned man made war,
And the ox-wain creaks o'er the burdened caves,
Where the mummied mammoths are.

Then, as we linger at luncheon here,
O'er many a dainty dish,
Let us drink anew to the time when you
Were a Tadpole and I was a Fish.

GIPSY-HEART

My grandsire was a vagabond
  Who made the Road his pride.
He left his son a wanderer's heart
  And little enough beside;
And all his life my father heard
The fluting of a hidden bird
That lured him on from hedge to hedge
  To walk the world so wide.

And now he walks the worlds beyond
  And drifts on hidden seas
Undesecrated by a chart —
  Blithe derelict at ease.
And sometimes when I halt at night —
In answer to my camp-fire's light
His own uplifts a glowing wedge
  Among the Pleiades.

Women are fair, but all too fond;
  Home holds a man too fast;
I 'll choose for mine a freeman's part,
  And sing as I go past.
No lighted windows beckon me,
The open sky my canopy,
I 'll camp upon Creation's edge
  A wanderer to the last.

THE HEART OF THE ROAD

I journey on an endless quest,
The eager miles are swift to run,
While up the hill and toward the west
My red leagues travel against the sun.

Behold, one journeyed in the night,
He sang amid the wind and rain;
My wet sands gave his feet delight.
When will that traveler come again?

Some house them with their kin inside,
Some habit to the ends of earth;
Strange is the heart of them that bide,
But I was a fugitive from birth.

The folk that tarry are not my sons;
My heart is all for them that roam;
My thought goes with the wandering ones
That spend the night from home.

The weary folk lead to and fro,
And he is dear that takes no rest;
Mine are those feet that come and go,
But, lo, my firstborn was my best!

" Heart of the Road," I heard him sing,
" Whose thought is swift, whose ways are wild,
The mother of my wandering
Shall have the pilgrim for her child."

How did he find me where I lay,
Remote, untraversed, and forespent?

How blithe I journey since the day
That he conceived the ways I went!

That day that he fared forth alone
His feet besought me in their need.
I cried out of my dust and stone,
" Lo, my own breast shall make thee bleed! "

I cried out from my rock and steep,
" My child, I cannot give thee rest! "
He moved the stone that grieved my sleep,
And soothed the sharp thorn from my breast.
Therefore my other sons are dear,
But still the firstborn is the best.

My will is in them night and day,
Men and the restless sons of men.
The paths are smooth wherein they stray.
When will that traveler come again?

Thick as the dust, from unborn years,
I see my coming children throng,
That one who breaks the way with tears
Many shall follow with a song.

Nor bread, nor scrip, nor staff had he
When he went out from the gray town.
Now heavy folk that traverse me
Burdened with wealth go up and down.

Each unto each I hear them call
With idle speech and empty boast,
And I have ease to give them all
Save him that I did love the most.

But when one passes in the night,
And tarries not by any door,
My leagues beat upward for delight, —
Perchance that traveler comes once more.

But when one journeys over me,
Nor staff, nor scrip, through wind and rain,
I reach my dim hands out to see
If those old feet have come again.

Therefore upon an endless quest
My eager miles are swift to run,
While up the hill and toward the west
My red leagues travel against the sun.

THE CRY OF THE DREAMER

I am tired of planning and toiling
    In the crowded hives of men,
Heart-weary of building and spoiling,
    And spoiling and building again,
And I long for the dear old river,
    Where I dreamed my youth away;
For a dreamer lives forever,
    And a toiler dies in a day.

I am sick of the showy seeming,
    Of life that is half a lie;
Of the faces lined with scheming
    In the throng that hurries by;
From the sleepless thought's endeavor
    I would go where the children play;
For a dreamer lives forever,
    And a thinker dies in a day.

I can feel no pride, but pity,
  For the burdens the rich endure;
There is nothing sweet in the city
  But the patient lives of the poor.
Oh, the little hands too skillful,
  And the child-mind choked with weeds!
The daughter's heart grown willful
  And the father's heart that bleeds!

No! no! from the streets' rude bustle,
  From trophies of mart and stage,
I would fly to the wood's low rustle
  And the meadows' kindly page.
Let me dream as of old by the river,
  And be loved for my dreams alway;
For a dreamer lives forever,
  And a toiler dies in a day.

THE JOURNEY

When he is hidden from the sun,
  And grasses grow where he is laid,
Men mark the good a man has done,
  And glorify the name he made.

Ay! Thus he spake and this his fame,
  And these the friends he loved to own;
'T was thus he played the goodly game,
  And now he wends his way — alone.

Oh, friend of mine, I shall not wait
  To sing when all save you may hear,
But in the noon of our estate,
  While yet the tide is strong and clear;

While wild March winds go staggering by;
— The lusty winds adventuring —
While to the shore the sea runs high
And life swells to the full, I sing!

I sing thy love the gray-green sea!
The wind that thunders in the sail!
The racing shadow on our lee!
And Romance laughing down the trail!

The shuddering rise, the plunging fall,
While through the storm far voices fling:
" Adventure was his coronal,
And all his wealth was wandering!"

What better life for thee and me:
The buffeting of wind and sun,
Hull-down upon the open sea,
And dreams unfolding, one by one?

The harbor of the broad lagoon,
The darkening shore, the early star,
The magic of the tropic moon,
New fortunes in a land afar?

And yet, if naught but dreams unfold,
As nameless from the sun we wend,
We 've coined them into singing gold,
And give them to the world to spend.

And when the last, long shadows fall,
May Romance o'er each dreamer sing;
" Adventure was his coronal,
And all his wealth was wandering!"

WANDERLUST

The birds were beating north again with faint and
  starry cries
Along their ancient highway that spans the mid-
  night skies,
And out across the rush of wings my heart went
  crying too,
Straight for the morning's windy walls and lakes
  of misted blue.

They gave me place among them, for well they
  understood
The magic wine of April working madness in my
  blood,
And we were kin in thought and dream as league
  by league together
We kept that pace of straining wings across the
  starry weather.

The dim blue tides of Fundy, green slopes of
  Labrador
Slid under us . . . our course was set for earth's
  remotest shore;
But tingling through the ether and searching star
  by star
A lonely voice went crying that drew me down
  from far.

Farewell, farewell, my brothers! I see you far
  away
Go drifting down the sunset across the last green
  bay,

But I have found the haven of this lonely heart and
    wild —
My falconer has called me — I am prisoned by a
    child.

THE KLONDIKE

Never mind the day we left, or the way the women
    clung to us;
All we need now is the last way they looked at us.
Never mind the twelve men there amid the cheer-
    ing —
Twelve men or one man, 't will soon be all the
    same;
For this is what we know; we are five men to-
    gether,
Five left o' twelve men to find the golden river.

Far we came to find it out, but the place was here
    for all of us;
Far, far we came, and here we have the last of us.
We that were the front men, we that would be
    early,
We that had the faith, and the triumph in our eyes:
We that had the wrong road, twelve men to-
    gether, —
Singing when the devil sang to find the golden
    river.

Say the gleam was not for us, but never say we
    doubted it;
Say the wrong road was right before we followed it.
We that were the front men, fit for all forage, —

Say that while we dwindle we are front men still;
For this is what we know to-night; we 're starving
        here together —
Starving on the wrong road to find the golden river.

Wrong, we say, but wait a little: hear him in the
        corner there;
He knows no more than we, and he 'll tell us if
        we 'll listen there —
He that fought the snow-sleep less than all the
        others
Stays awhile yet, and he knows where he stays:
Foot and hand a frozen clout, brain a freezing
        feather,
Still he 's here to talk with us and to the golden river.

"Flow," he says, " and flow along, but you cannot
        flow away from us;
All the world's ice will never keep you far from us;
Every man that heeds your call takes the way that
        leads him —
The one way that 's his way, and lives his own life;
Starve or laugh, the game goes on, and on goes the
        river;
Gold or no, they go their way — twelve men to-
        gether.

"Twelve," he says, " who sold their shame for a
        lure you call too fair for them —
You that laugh and flow to the same word that
        urges them:
Twelve who left the old town shining in the sunset,
Left the weary street and the small safe days;

Twelve who knew but one way out, wide the way
    or narrow:
Twelve who took the frozen chance and laid their
    lives on yellow.

" Flow by night and flow by day, nor ever once be
    seen by them;
Flow, freeze, and flow, till time shall hide the
    bones of them;
Laugh and wash their names away, leave them all
    forgotten,
Leave the old town to crumble where it sleeps;
Leave it there as they have left it, shining in the
    valley, —
Leave the town to crumble down and let the
    women marry.

" Twelve of us or five," he says, " we know the
    night is on us now:
Five while we last, and we may as well be thinking
    now:
Thinking each his own thought, knowing, when
    the light comes,
Five left or none left, the game will not be lost.
Crouch or sleep, we go the way, the last way to-
    gether:
Five or none, the game goes on, and on goes the
    river.

" For after all that we have done and all that we
    have failed to do,
Life will be life and the world will have its work
    to do:

Every man who follows us will heed in his own
    fashion
The calling and the warning and the friends who
    do not know:
Each will hold an icy knife to punish his heart's
    lover,
And each will go the frozen way to find the golden
    river."

There you hear him, all he says, and the last we 'll
    ever get of him.
Now he wants to sleep, and that will be the best
    for him.
Let him have his own way — no, you need n't
    shake him —
Your own turn will come, so let the man sleep.
For this is what we know: we are stalled here to-
    gether —
Hands and feet and hearts of us, to find the golden
    river.

And there 's a quicker way than sleep? . . . Never
    mind the looks of him:
All he needs now is a finger on the eyes of him.
You there on the left hand, reach a little over —
Shut the stars away, or he 'll see them all night:
He 'll see them all night and he 'll see them all to-
    morrow,
Crawling down the frozen sky, cold and hard and
    yellow.

Won't you move an inch or two — to keep the
    stars away from him?
— No, he won't move, and there 's no need of ask-
    ing him.

Never mind the twelve men, never mind the
    women;
Three while we last, we 'll let them all go;
And we 'll hold our thoughts north while we starve
    here together,
Looking each his own way to find the golden river.

THE LAST TRAIL

(TO JACK LONDON)

Nay, it shall never be
That sombre requiems are tolled for thee!
But there shall be wild music from the shore
Of flowering Wai-ki-ki; and when the door
Of Morn opes wide upon blue Frisco Bay,
Then let a rollicking fo'c'sle song
Be lilted loud and long
To cheer thee, comrade, on thy shadowy way.
See! where, above the pines, snow clouds are drift-
    ing —
And Nome's white lights grow weary with the dawn.
Hark thou the sledge-dog drivers calling, calling,
While winter's chains are falling.
'T is thee they mark, old comrade, thee they hail
With " Musha! Musha!" down the Sitka trail.
But hush! — the wind from off the Yukon 's shift-
    ing,
And thou must hasten on!

Thou wert indeed adventurous with life —
Yea, life was but adventure keen for thee,
Ev'n as Ulysses on the moonless sea.
Like Jason, too, thou sawest much of strife,

Yet camest home at last
From all thy journeys vast,
To domesticity.

O King of proud adventure, fare thee well!
Master of silver words with tales to tell,
May thou by day have hunter's winey zest,
And by thy nightly campfire, happy rest,
Whether through sun or rain or snow-lashed gale,
On this which is for thee the last —
The Unknown Trail.

THE LAST OF ALL

Whether it's Heaven — or whether it's Hell,
　　Or whether it's merely sleep;
Or whether it's something in between
　　Where ghosts of the half-gods creep;
Since it comes at once — and it comes to all —
　　On the one, fixed, certain date —
Why drink of the dregs till the Cup arrives
　　On the gray day set by Fate?

The coward looks to the gray beyond
　　And his heart grows white with fear;
The dark is deep that he may not see
　　As the end of the game draws near;
But the valiant turns to another road
　　That leads to the outbound gates,
Where each drab soul of the realm must fare
　　And the Great Adventure waits.

One by one till the line is passed —
　　The gutter-born and the crown;

So what is a day or a year or two
  Since the answer's written down?
What is a day to a million years
  When the last winds sound the call?
So here's to the days that rest between —
  And here's to the last of all!

THE LAST JOURNEY

I felt the world a-spinning on its nave,
  I felt it sheering blindly round the sun;
I felt the time had come to find a grave:
  I knew it in my heart my days were done.
I took my staff in hand: I took the road,
And wandered out to seek my last Abode.
    Hearts of gold and hearts of lead,
      Sing it yet in sun and rain,
    "Heel and toe from dawn to dusk,
      Round the world and home again."

  .   .   .   .

My feet are heavy now, but on I go,
  My head erect beneath the tragic years.
The way is steep, but I would have it so;
  And dusty, but I lay the dust with tears,
Though none can see me weep: alone I climb
The rugged path that leads me out of time —
    Out of time and out of all,
      Singing yet in sun and rain,
    "Heel and toe from dawn to dusk,
      Round the world and home again."

Farewell, the hope that mocked, farewell despair
  That went before me still and made the pace.

The earth is full of graves, and mine was there
  Before my life began, my resting-place;
And I shall find it out and with the dead
Lie down for ever, all my sayings said.
  Deeds all done, songs all sung,
    While others chant in sun and rain,
" Heel and toe from dawn to dusk,
    Round the world and home again."

BATTLE-CRY

More than half-beaten, but fearless,
Facing the storm and the night;
Breathless and reeling, but tearless,
Here in the lull of the fight,
I who bow not but before Thee,
God of the fighting clan,
Lifting my fists I implore Thee,
Give me the heart of a Man!

What though I live with the winners
Or perish with those who fall?
Only the cowards are sinners,
Fighting the fight is all.
Strong is my Foe — he advances!
Snapt is my blade, O Lord!
See the proud banners and lances!
Oh spare me this stub of a sword!

Give me no pity, nor spare me;
Calm not the wrath of my Foe.
See where he beckons to dare me!
Bleeding, half beaten — I go.

Not for the glory of winning,
Not for the fear of the night;
Shunning the battle is sinning —
Oh spare me the heart to fight!

Red is the mist about me;
Deep is the wound in my side;
"Coward!" thou criest to flout me?
O terrible Foe, thou hast lied!
Here with my battle before me,
God of the fighting clan,
Grant that the woman who bore me
Suffered to suckle a man!

IMPENITENTIA ULTIMA

Before my light goes out forever if God should give
    me choice of graces,
I would not reck of length of days, nor crave for
    things to be;
But cry: "One day of the great lost days, one face
    of all the faces,
Grant me to see and touch once more and nothing
    more to see.

"For, Lord, I was free of all Thy flowers, but I
    chose the world's sad roses,
And that is why my feet are torn and mine eyes are
    blind with sweat,
But at Thy terrible judgment-seat when this my
    tired life closes,
I am ready to reap whereof I sowed and pay my
    righteous debt.

"But once before the sand is run and the silver
    thread is broken,
Give me a grace and cast aside the veil of dolorous
    years,
Grant me one hour of all mine hours and let me see
    for a token
Her pure and pitiful eyes shine out and bathe her
    feet with tears."

Her pitiful hands should calm and her hair stream
    down and blind me.
Out of the sight of night and out of the reach of
    fear,
And her eyes should be my light whilst the sun
    went out behind me,
And the viols in her voice be the last sound in mine
    ear.

Before the ruining waters fall and my life be car-
    ried under,
And Thine anger cleave me through as a child cuts
    down a flower,
I will praise Thee, Lord, in Hell, while my limbs are
    racked asunder,
For the last sad sight of her face and the little grace
    of an hour.

THE GLORIOUS FOOL

Christ save me from half-hearted men,
    Who time their steps by hour and rule;
Who measure life by word and pen,
    Too pale of mind to play the fool.

For me, the glorious fool who rides,
  High poised upon the neck of Fate;
Who laughs when palsied censure chides;
  Who dares to love — and dares to hate.

Oh, fool, on your adventure-trail
  That flames across the farthest wave,
The storm that thunders in your sail,
  The tide that swings above your grave,

Stars mirrored in the dreamless sea,
  White faces of the loves you knew,
Great-hearted men who dare be free,
  Chant deathless requiem to you!

Captain of causes lost, forlorn,
  Drunk with the glory of the strife,
You faced with joy each fighting morn,
  Full-throated, drinking deep of life.

Mad lover, striding overbold
  Through uncompanioned, loveless years,
Still are you victor! Still you hold
  The memory of those lips, those tears.

Atom of star-fire lightly tossed
  To the abysmal maw of Time,
Wise men forgathering, whisper, " Lost! "
  But to their hearts they cry, " Sublime! "

And I? Ah, would that I might these
  Rude stanzas shape to worth and rule;
But like to you, I may not please
  Half-hearted men, Oh, glorious fool!

THE SPELL OF THE YUKON

I wanted the gold, and I sought it;
　　I scrabbled and mucked like a slave.
Was it famine or scurvy — I fought it;
　　I hurled my youth into a grave.
I wanted the gold, and I got it —
　　Came out with a fortune last fall, —
Yet somehow life 's not what I thought it,
　　And somehow the gold is n't all.

No! There 's the land — (have you seen it?)
　　It 's the cussedest land that I know,
From the big, dizzy mountains that screen it
　　To the deep, deathlike valleys below.
Some say God was tired when He made it;
　　Some say it 's a fine land to shun;
Maybe; but there 's some as would trade it
　　For no land on earth — and I 'm one.

You come to get rich (damned good reason);
　　You feel like an exile at first;
You hate it like hell for a season,
　　And then you are worse than the worst.
It grips you like some kinds of sinning;
　　It twists you from foe to a friend;
It seems it 's been since the beginning;
　　It seems it will be to the end.

I 've stood in some mighty-mouthed hollow
　　That 's plumb-full of hush to the brim;
I 've watched the big, husky sun wallow
　　In crimson and gold, and grow dim,

Till the moon set the pearly peaks gleaming,
   And the stars tumbled out, neck and crop;
And I thought that I surely was dreaming,
   With the peace o' the world piled on top.

The summer — no sweeter was ever;
   The sunshiny woods all athrill;
The grayling aleap in the river,
   The bighorn asleep on the hill.
The strong life that never knows harness;
   The wilds where the caribou call;
The freshness, the freedom, the farness —
   O God! how I'm stuck on it all!

The winter! the brightness that blinds you,
   The white land locked tight as a drum,
The cold fear that follows and finds you,
   The silence that bludgeons you dumb.
The snows that are older than history,
   The woods where the weird shadows slant;
The stillness, the moonlight, the mystery,
   I've bade 'em good-by — but I can't.

There's a land where the mountains are name-
   less,
   And the rivers all run God knows where;
There are lives that are erring and aimless,
   And deaths that just hang by a hair;
There are hardships that nobody reckons;
   There are valleys unpeopled and still;
There's a land — oh, it beckons and beckons,
   And I want to go back — and I will.

They 're making my money diminish;
   I 'm sick of the taste of champagne.
Thank God! when I 'm skinned to a finish
   I 'll pike to the Yukon again.
I 'll fight — and you bet it 's no sham-fight;
   It 's hell! — but I 've been there before;
And it 's better than this by a damsight —
   So me for the Yukon once more.

There 's gold, and it 's haunting and haunting;
   It 's luring me on as of old;
Yet it is n't the gold that I 'm wanting
   So much as just finding the gold.
It 's the great, big, broad land 'way up yonder,
   It 's the forests where silence has lease;
It 's the beauty that thrills me with wonder,
   It 's the stillness that fills me with peace.

THE LITTLE FIRES

From East to West they 're burning, in forge and
   tower and home,
And on beyond the outlands, across the ocean-
   foam;
In far and misty islands; o'er plain and sea and
   height,
The little fires along the trail that twinkle down
   the night.

There 's the camp-fire of the hobo, beside the
   trestle beam;
Where he crouches by a smoky can and dreams a
   hazy dream;

The trestle creaks and quivers beneath the mid-
    night mail,
Oh, he 'll follow it to-morrow — sifting down the
    iron trail,

Adventuring! Adventuring! and oh, the sights to
    see,
And little fires along the trail that wink at you and
    me.

With a thousand miles behind us and a thousand
    miles to go,
We 'll turn and cross the mesa where encircled by
    a glow,
There 's a cattle-trail to water and a belted cow-
    boy crew,
And the canvas of the wagon with the shadows
    trembling through;

And a whole and hearty welcome in each voice
    and eye and hand;
— An outfit on the round-up, glad of news from
    overland —
Sit right in and tell your story, sing your song or
    eat your chuck;
Here 's a health in red-hot coffee; " To the trail —
    and plenty luck! "

Adventuring! Adventuring! and oh, the sights to
    see!
And little fires in bronco eyes that wink at you and
    me.

Where the mesa meets the timber as it marches
    up the steep,
Glows a beacon like a hill-star near a band of
    bedded sheep;
From the firelight's fading circle where the sheep
    and shadows blend,
"Como'sta, amigo!" greets you — Spanish for
    "How goes it, friend?"

And the Andalusian herder curls a smoke and
    points the way,
As he murmurs, Caliente, San Clemente, Santa Fé,
Till the very words are music waking memoried
    desires,
And you turn and foot it down the trail to find more
    little fires.

Adventuring! Adventuring! and oh, the sights to see!
And little fires of Southern stars that wink at you
    and me.

The wind from down the ranges whispers out
    across the sand,
And who would think to find a fire in this forgot-
    ten land?
Yet in the desert spaces a tiny ember gleams
And by the fire a wanderer, asleep in splendid
    dreams;

Dreams of gold he 'll find to-morrow, but the vain
    to-morrows come,
Till the heart has ceased its singing and the lips
    of hope are dumb;

Till a phantom figure, rising, with a phantom burro,
    plods
Out across the mighty silence seeking golden altar-
    gods;

Adventuring! Adventuring! and oh, the sights to
    see!
And little, hidden, yellow fires that wink at you and
    me.

Up the mountain, down the valley to the sleepy
    harbor side,
Where a score of lights are blinking and a schooner
    waits the tide,
Where a dripping dory beckons as the ruddy shad-
    ows dance,
Down a trail that 's ever leading to the islands of
    Romance;

Till the last adventure calls us from the old, the
    vain desires,
To a way that 's still untrodden, though aglow with
    little fires,
Where no wanderer grows weary and a man is
    free to roam,
Or hang his hat upon a star and call the planet
    " Home! "

EARTH-BORN

No lapidary's heaven, no brazier's hell for me,
For I am made of dust and dew and stream and
    plant and tree;

I 'm close akin to boulders, I am cousin to the
    mud,
And all the winds of all the skies make music in my
    blood.

I want a brook and pine trees, I want a storm to
    blow
Loud-lunged across the looming hills with rain and
    sleet and snow;
Don't put me off with diadems and thrones of
    chrysoprase, —
I want the winds of northern nights and wild March
    days.

My blood runs red with sunset, my body is white
    with rain,
And on my heart auroral skies have set their scarlet
    stain,
My thoughts are green with spring time, among the
    meadow rue
I think my very soul is growing green and gold and
    blue.

What will be left, I wonder, when Death has washed
    me clean
Of dust and dew and sundown and April's virgin
    green?
If there 's enough to make a ghost, I 'll bring it
    back again
To the little lovely earth that bore me, body, soul,
    and brain.

ROAD SONG

Give me the clear blue sky overhead, and the long
    road to my feet,
And the winds of heaven to winnow me through,
    and a brother tramp to greet,
With an inn at the end of day for rest, and the world
    may keep its bays —
For these are the gifts of the wayside gods, and the
    gifts that I would praise.

Come from the murk of your city streets to the tent
    of all the world,
When your final word on Art is said, and your flag
    of Faith is furled,
When your heart no longer gives a throb at the first
    faint breath of Spring —
Ah, turn your feet to the ribbon-road with a chorus
    all may sing!

Where the sandalled Dawn like a Greek god takes
    the hurdles of the hills,
And the brooding earth rubs sleepy eyes at the song
    some lone bird trills,
Where a brook, like a silver scythe of the moon,
    awaits your warm caress —
Ah, these are the gifts that the High Gods fling to
    mortals in duress!

When the blood-red sun swings low in the west, and
    an end comes to Desire,
When the candle-gloom of the low-ceiled room is
    bared to a pine log fire,

And the tales of men are told anew till the Huntress
leaves the sky —
Ah, these are the gifts for the sons of men to set
their treasure by!

Then give me the clear blue sky overhead, and the
long road to my feet,
And a dog to tell my secrets to, and a brother tramp
to meet —
And the years may take their toll of me till I come
to the weary West,
And I lodge for good in the world's own inn, a way-
worn, waiting guest!

DESERTED ROADS

Time was we sang of wanderers who trod the open
trail
And roved about the merry world by foot or train or
sail,
Who knew the wind-swept spaces and who braved
the sun and rain,
Or followed gypsy caravans by mountain peak or
plain.

But now the roads are empty of the blithe and
restless clan,
And bats and owls are resting in the idle gypsy
van;
For every true adventurer who never could be
still
Has joined the greatest game of all and found a
keener thrill.

They're somewhere in the trenches and they're
    somewhere in the air;
Oh, look along the battle line and you will find
    them there,
But when the war is over and we welcome back our
    men,
The rovers — what are left of them — will hit the
    trail again.

THE HORSE THIEF

There he moved, cropping the grass at the purple
    canyon's lip.
    His mane was mixed with the moonlight that
        silvered his snow-white side,
For the moon sailed out of a cloud with the wake of
    a spectral ship,
    I crouched and crawled on my belly, with my
        lariat coil looped wide.

Dimly and dark the mesas broke on the starry
    sky.
    A pall covered every color of their gorgeous
        glory at noon.
I smelt the yucca and mesquite, and stifled my
    heart's quick cry,
    And wormed and crawled on my belly to where
        he moved against the moon.

Some Moorish barb was that mustang's sire. His
    lines were beyond all wonder
    From the prick of his ears to the flow of his tail
        he ached in my throat and eyes.

Steel and velvet grace! As the prophet says, God
    had " clothed his neck with thunder."
  Oh, marvelous with the drifting cloud he drifted
    across the skies!

And then I was near at hand — crouched and bal-
    anced and cast the coil;
  And the moon was smothered in cloud, and the
    rope through my hands with a rip!
But somehow I gripped and clung, with the blood
    in my brain a-boil, —
  With a turn round the rugged tree-stump there
    on the canyon's lip.

Right into the stars he reared aloft, his red eye
    rolling and raging.
  He whirled and sunfished and lashed, and rocked
    the earth to thunder and flame.
He squealed like a regular devil-horse. I was
    haggard and spent and aging —
  Roped clean, but almost storming clear, his fury
    too fierce to tame.

And I cursed myself for a tenderfoot moon-daz-
    zled to play the part,
  But I was doubly desperate then, with the posse
    pulled out from town,
Or I'd never have tried it. I only knew I must get
    a mount and start.
  The filly had snapped her foreleg short. I had
    had to shoot her down.

So there he struggled and strangled, and I snubbed
    him around the tree.
  Nearer, a little nearer — hoofs planted, and loll-
    ing tongue —
Till a sudden slack pitched me backward. He
    reared right on top of me.
  Mother of God — that moment! He missed me
    — and up I swung.

Somehow — gone daft completely and clawing a
    bunch of his mane,
  As he stumbled and tripped in the lariat, there
    I was — up and astride
And cursing for seven counties! And the mustang?
    Just insane!
  Crack-bang! went the rope; we cannoned off the
    tree — then — gods, that ride!

A rocket — that's all — a rocket! I dug with my
    teeth and nails.
  Why we never hit even the high spots (though I
    hardly remember things),
But I heard a monstrous booming like a thunder
    of flapping sails
  When he spread — well, *call* me a liar! — when
    he spread those wings, those wings!

So white that my eyes were blinded, thick-feath-
    ered and wide unfurled,
  They beat the air into billows. We sailed, and
    the earth was gone.

Canyon and desert and mesa withered below, with
    the world.
  And then I knew that mustang; for I — was
    Bellerophon!

Yes, glad as the Greek, and mounted on a horse
    of the elder gods,
  With never a magic bridle or a fountain-mir-
    ror nigh!
My chaps and spurs and holster must have looked it?
    What's the odds?
  I'd a leg over lightning and thunder careering
    across the sky!

And forever streaming before me, fanning my fore-
    head cool,
  Flowed a mane of molten silver; and just before
    my thighs
(As I gripped his velvet-muscled ribs, while I
    cursed myself for a fool),
  The steady pulse of those pinions — their won-
    derful fall and rise!

The bandanna I bought in Bowie blew loose and
    whipped from my neck.
  My shirt was stuck to my shoulders and ribbon-
    ing out behind.
The stars were dancing, wheeling and glancing,
    dipping with smirk and beck
  The clouds were flowing, dusking and glowing.
    We rode a roaring wind.

We soared through the silver starlight to knock
    at the planets' gates.
  New shimmering constellations came whirling
    into our ken.
Red stars and green and golden swung out of the
    void that waits
  For man's great last adventure; the signs took
    shape — and then

I knew the lines of that Centaur the moment I
    saw him come!
  The musical-box of the heavens all round us
    rolled to a tune
That tinkled and chimed and trilled with silver
    sounds that struck you dumb,
  As if some archangel were grinding out the music
    of the moon.

Melody-drunk on the Milky Way as we swept and
    soared hilarious,
  Full in our pathway sudden he stood — the
    Centaur of the stars,
Flashing from head and hoofs and breast! I knew
    him for Sagittarius.
  He reared and bent and drew his bow. He
    crouched as a boxer spars.

Flung back on his haunches, weird he loomed —
    then leapt — and the dim void lightened.
  Old White Wings shied and swerved aside and
    fled from the splendor-shod.

Through a flashing welter of worlds we charged.
    I knew why my horse was frightened.
    He *had* two faces — a dog's and a man's — that
        Babylonian god!

Also, he followed us real as fear. Ping! went an
    arrow past.
    My bronco buck-jumped, humping high. We
        plunged . . . I guess that 's all!
I lay on the purple canyon's lip, when I opened my
    eyes at last —
    Stiff and sore and my head like a drum, but I
        broke no bones in the fall.

So you know — and now you may string me up.
    Such was the way you have caught me.
    Thank you for letting me tell it straight, though
        you never could greatly care.
For I took a horse that was n't mine! . . . But
    there 's one the heavens brought me,
    And I 'll hang right happy because I know he is
        waiting for me up there.

From creamy muzzle to cannon-bone, by God, he 's
    a peerless wonder!
    He is steel and velvet and furnace-fire, and
        death's supremest prize;
And never again shall be roped on earth that neck
    that is " clothed with thunder." . . .
    String me up, Dave! Go dig my grave. *I rode him
    across the skies!*

WHEN THE DRIVE GOES DOWN

There 's folks that like the good dry land, an' folks
    that like the sea,
But rock an' river, shoal an' sand, are good enough
    for me.
There 's folks that like the ocean crest, an' folks
    that like the town —
But when I really feel the best is when the drive
    goes down.
        So pole away, you river rats,
          From landin' down to lake —
        There 's miles of pine to keep in line,
          A hundred jams to break!

There 's folks that like to promenade along the
    boulevard,
But here 's a spot I would n't trade for all their
    pavement hard;
Ten thousand lawgs by currents birled an' waters
    white that hiss —
Oh, where 's the sidewalk in the world that 's half
    as fine as this?
        So leap away, you river rats,
          From landin' down to sluice;
        There 's lawgs to run, there 's peavy fun
          To break the timber loose!

An' ev'ry rollin' of a stick that starts her down the
    stream
An' ev'ry bit of water quick where runnin' ripples
    gleam

Means gittin' nearer to the end, to wife an' babe
an' rest —
An' ev'ry time you turn a bend the next bend looks
the best.
    Then peg away, you river rats,
      From sluiceway down to mill —
      Each rock you clear will bring you near
      The house upon the hill!

There 's folks that like the good dry land, an' folks
that like the sea,
But rock an' river, shoal an' sand, are good enough
for me.
There 's folks that like the ocean crest, an' folks
that like the town —
But when I really feel the best is when the drive
goes down!

THE LITTLE RED GOD

Here 's a little red song to the god of guts,
Who dwells in palaces, brothels, huts;
The little Red God with the craw of grit;
The god who never learned how to quit;
He is neither a fool with a frozen smile,
Or a sad old toad in a cask of bile;
He can dance with a shoe-nail in his heel
And never a sign of his pain reveal;
He can hold a mob with an empty gun
And turn a tragedy into fun;
Kill a man in a flash, a breath,
Or snatch a friend from the claws of death;
Swallow the pill of assured defeat

And plan attack in his slow retreat;
Spin the wheel till the numbers dance,
And bite his thumb at the god of Chance;
Drink straight water with whisky-soaks,
Or call for liquor with temperance folks;
Tearless stand at the graven stone,
Yet weep in the silence of night, alone;
Worship a sweet, white virgin's glove,
Or teach a courtesan how to love;
Dare the dulness of fireside bliss,
Or stake his soul for a wanton's kiss;
Blind his soul to a woman's eyes
When she says she loves and he knows she
   lies;
Shovel dung in the city mart
To earn a crust for his chosen art;
Build where the builders all have failed,
And sail the seas that no man has sailed;
Run a tunnel or dam a stream,
Or damn the men who financed the dream;
Tell a pal what his work is worth,
Though he lose his last, best friend on earth;
Lend the critical monkey-elf
A razor — hoping he 'll kill himself;
Wear the garments he likes to wear,
Never dreaming that people stare;
Go to church if his conscience wills,
Or find his own — in the far, blue hills.

He is kind and gentle, or harsh and gruff;
He is tender as love — or he 's rawhide tough;
A rough-necked rider in spurs and chaps,
Or well-groomed son of the town — perhaps;

And this is the little Red God I sing,
Who cares not a wallop for anything
That walks or gallops, that crawls or struts,
No matter how clothed — if it has n't guts.

HAMISH

A Scotch Terrier

Little lad, little lad, and who's for an airing,
Who's for the river and who's for a run;
Four little pads to go fitfully faring,
Looking for trouble and calling it fun?
Down in the sedges the water-rats revel,
Up in the wood there are bunnies at play
With a weather-eye wide for a Little Black Devil;
But the Little Black Devil won't come to-day.

To-day at the farm the ducks may slumber,
To-day may the tabbies an anthem raise;
Rat and rabbit beyond all number
To-day untroubled, go their ways;
To-day is an end of the shepherd's labour,
No more will the sheep be hunted astray;
And the Irish terrier, foe and neighbour,
Says, " What 's old Hamish about to-day? "

Ay, what indeed? In the nether spaces
Will the soul of a Little Black Dog despair?
Will the Quiet Folk scare him with shadow-faces?
And how will he tackle the Strange Beasts there?
Tail held high, I 'll warrant, and bristling,
Marching stoutly if sore afraid,
Padding it steadily, softly whistling; —
That's how the Little Black Devil was made.

Then well-a-day for a " cantie callant,"
A heart of gold and a soul of glee, —
Sportsman, gentleman, squire and gallant, —
Teacher, maybe, of you and me.
Spread the turf on him light and level,
Grave him a headstone clear and true —
" Here lies Hamish, the Little Black Devil,
And half of the heart of his mistress too."

THE WALKING MAN

Sunny summer day it was when loping in to Laramie,
   I overtook the Walking Man, reined up and
      nodded " How! "
He 'd been a rider once, I knew. He smiled, but
      scarce aware of me,
   He said, " If you would like me to, I 'll tell my
      story, now.

" They 'll tell you that I 'm crazy — that my wits
      have gone to glory,
   But you must n't be believing every Western
      yarn you hear.
The one I 'm going to tell you is exceptional —
      a story
   That you 've heard perhaps a dozen ways a dozen
      times a year."

So he whispered while the shadow of my pony
      walked beside him,
   " If good people go to heaven, do good horses go
      to hell ? "

I slung one leg across the horn and sideways so, I
    eyed him;
  " For I 've seen the phantom ponies loping round
    the Big Corral.

" And I 've seen my pony Yuma — yes, the horse
    that died to save me —
  Come and nicker at the golden bars while I stood
    down below
Calling, ' Yuma! Yuma! Yuma! ' and still wonder-
    ing why He gave me
  Such a friend; and why I killed her. It was
    twenty years ago. . . .

" You remember; it was lonely when we used to
    guard the cattle;
  When a man would ride the line for days and
    camp at night alone,
With nothing much to do but watch the sun rise up
    for battle,
  And not a soul to talk to, or what 's even worse —
    his own.

" So I taught my pony Yuma many tricks, for she
    was human;
  To rear, shake hands, to nod, or pick up anything
    I dropped,
Till she grew as interested and as gentle as a
    woman,
  Just to have me praise and pet her; but one day
    the teaching stopped.

" Three rustlers from the Notch rode up. I knew
    there would be trouble,
  But I sat my pony easy and I rolled a cigarette,
And we talked about the *rodeo*, when, like a burst-
    ing bubble,
    The leader opened up the fight. I felt my arm
    grow wet. . . .

" It was three to one; but Yuma, like a rock, stood
    to the thunder,
    For she seemed to know my need. . . . Two
    empty saddles . . . when the one
That tried at first to get me spurred up close and
    swung up under,
    And I saw the trail to heaven in the muzzle of his
    gun.

" I flinched and played the coward. ' Up! ' I called,
    and at the calling
    Reared my pony; and she took his shot. I leveled
    quick and twice
I answered. In the smoke I saw a twisted figure
    falling;
    I could feel my pony shiver. . . . Twenty years
    I 've paid the price

" For my life. Yes, Hell-and-Texas leave the hoof-
    prints in some faces;
    We, the riders of the ranges, each of us have
    played his part. . . .
Twenty years! " he whispered slowly, " Twenty
    years in many places,
    But I 've never worn the print of Yuma's hoof-
    marks from my heart.

" I 'm the Walking Man forever. But I dream of
        mighty ranges
    And the silent mountain-meadows in the glory
        of the stars;
And I see the phantom ponies in the dawn and sun-
        set changes,
    And I hear my Yuma nicker, just behind the
        golden bars."

Sunny summer day it was when loping in to
        Laramie,
    I overtook the Walking Man, reined up and
        nodded " How ! "
He walked beside me for a while. He hardly was
        aware of me,
    But I think I understand him, for I know his
        story now.

THE BRONCO THAT WOULD NOT BE
BROKEN OF DANCING

A little colt-bronco, loaned to the farm
To be broken in time without fury or harm,
Yet black crows flew past you, shouting alarm.
Calling, " Beware ! " with lugubrious singing.
But the butterflies there in the bush were romanc-
        ing,
The smell of the grass caught your soul in a
        trance,
So why be a-fearing the spurs and the traces,
O bronco that would not be broken of dancing?

You were born with the pride of the lords great and
     olden
Who danced through the ages in corridors golden.
In all the wide farm-place the person most human.
You spoke out so plainly with squealing and caper-
     ing,
With whinnying, snorting, contorting and pranc-
     ing,
As you dodged your pursuers, looking askance,
With Greek-footed figures and Parthenon paces,
O bronco that would not be broken of dancing.

The grasshoppers cheered. "Keep whirling," they
     said.
The insolent sparrow called from the shed,
" If men will not laugh, make them wish they were
     dead."
But arch were your thoughts, all malice displacing.
Though the horse-killers came with snake-whips
     advancing,
You bantered and cantered away your last chance.
And they scourged you with Hell in their speech
     and their faces,
O bronco that would not be broken of dancing.

" Nobody cares for you," rattled the crows,
As you dragged the whole reaper, next day, down
     the rows.
The three mules held back yet you danced on your
     toes.
You pulled like a racer and kept the mules chasing,
You tangled the harness with bright eyes side-
     glancing,

While the drunk driver bled you, a pole for a lance,
And the giant mules bit at you, keeping their places,
O bronco that would not be broken of dancing.

In the last afternoon your boyish heart broke.
The hot wind came down like a sledge-hammer
       stroke.
The blood-sucking flies to a rare feast awoke.
And they searched out your wounds, your death-
       warrant tracing;
And the merciful men, their religion enhancing,
Stopped the red reaper to give you a chance.
Then you died on the prairie, and scorned all dis-
       graces,
O bronco that would not be broken of dancing.

REQUIEM

Under the wide and starry sky
Dig the grave and let me lie.
Glad did I live and gladly die,
And I laid me down with a will.

This be the verse you grave for me:
Here he lies where he longed to be;
Home is the sailor, home from the sea,
And the hunter home from the hill.

BOOT HILL

Go softly, you whose careless feet
Would crush the sage-brush, pungent sweet,
And brush the rabbit weed aside
From burrows where the ground squirrels hide,

And prairie dog his watch tower keeps
Among the ragged gravel heaps.
Year long the wind blows up and down
Each lessening mound, and drifts the brown,
Dried wander-weed there at their feet —
Who no more wander, slow or fleet.
Sun-bleached, rain-warped, the headboards hold
One story, all too quickly told:
That here some wild heart takes its rest
From spent desire and fruitless quest.

Here in the greasewood's scanty shade
How many a daring soul was laid!
Boots on, full-garbed as when he died;
The pistol belted at his side;
The worn sombrero on his breast —
To prove another man the best.
Arrow or knife or quick-drawn gun —
The glad, mad, fearless game was done;
A life for stakes — play slow or fast —
Win — lose — yet Death was trumps at last.

Some went where bar-room tinsel flared,
Or painted dance-hall wantons stared;
Some, where the lone, brown ranges bared
Their parched length to a parching sky,
And God alone might hear the cry
From thirst-dried lips that stiff and cold
Seemed still to babble: " Gold! Gold! Gold! "
Woman or wine or greed or Chance —
A comrade's shot, an Indian lance;
By camp or canyon, trail or street —
Here all games end; here all trails meet.

The ground squirrels chatter in the sun;
The dry, gray sage-leaves one by one,
Drift down, close-curled, in odorous heaps;
Above, side-winged, a wild hawk sweeps;
And on the worn board at the head
Of one whose name was fear and dread,
A little, solemn ground owl sits.
Ah, here the man and life are quits!
Go softly, nor with careless feet —
Here all games end; here all trails meet.

THE SEXTON'S INN

Only a little longer,
  And the journey is done, my friend!
Only a little further,
  And the road will have an end!
The shadows begin to lengthen,
  The evening soon will close,
And its ho! for the Inn of the Sexton —
  The inn where we 'll all repose.

The inn has no bridal chamber,
  No suites for the famed or great;
The guests when they go to slumber
  Are all of the same estate;
The chambers are small and narrow,
  The couches are hard and cold,
And the grinning, fleshless landlord
  Is not to be bribed with gold.

A sheet for the proud and haughty,
  A sheet for the beggar guest,

A sheet for the blooming maiden —
    A sheet for us all, and — rest!
No bells at the dawn of morning,
    No rap at the chamber door;
But silence is there, and slumber,
    For ever and evermore.

Envoi

Then ho! for the Inn of the Sexton,
    The Inn where we all must sleep,
When our hands are done with toiling
And our eyes have ceased to weep.

RIDING AT NIGHT

On and on through the silent night,
Under the sky with its tranquil light
Of stars that are smiling and blinking bright —
    Riding . . . just riding along . . .

Up the hill and over the rise;
Can't see the trail but my horse is wise;
He knows where the hidden hill-trail lies;
    Riding . . . just riding along . . .

A flicker of fire from his steel-shod feet,
As the hoof-beats ring and the rocks repeat —
Easy, boy! Easy! Now keep your feet;
    Riding . . . just riding along . . .

Out of the stillness, faint and small,
The lean, gray hunters of midnight call,
And the querulous echoes rise and fall;
    Riding . . . just riding along . . .

The trail of a meteor streaks the sky,
And drops in the void of the dusk to die,
And I gaze as I wonder, " Where — and Why?"
    Riding . . . just riding along . . .

The jingle of rein-chains seems to be
Singing a song of peace to me;
A song of the range where a man is free . . .
    Riding . . . just riding along . . .

And the white moon rising above the gap,
Smiles on the world in its quiet nap,
Dreaming away in old Nature's lap;
    Riding . . . just riding along . . .

Then the crest of the range is a rose-lit height,
As the dawn leaps after the fading night,
And we 're back in camp with the morning light;
    Riding . . . just riding along . . .

THE PLAINSMEN

Men of the older, gentler soil,
  Loving the things that their fathers wrought —
Worn old fields of their fathers' toil,
  Scarred old hills where their fathers fought —
Loving their land for each ancient trace,
Like a mother dear for her wrinkled face,
  Such as they never can understand
  The way we have loved you, young, young land!

Born of a free, world-wandering race,
  Little we yearned o'er an oft-turned sod.

What did we care for the father's place,
  Having ours fresh from the hand of God?
Who feared the strangeness or wiles of you
When, from the unreckoned miles of you,
  Thrilling the wind with a sweet command,
  Youth unto youth called, young, young land?

North, where the hurrying seasons changed
  Over great gray plains where the trails lay long,
Free as the sweeping Chinook we ranged,
  Setting our days to a saddle-song.
Through the icy challenge you flung to us,
Through your shy Spring kisses that clung to us,
  Following far as the rainbow spanned,
  Fiercely we wooed you, young, young land.

South, where the sullen black mountains guard
  Limitless, shimmering lands of the sun,
Over blinding trails where the hoofs rang hard,
  Laughing or cursing we rode and won.
Drunk with the virgin white fire of you,
Hotter than thirst was desire of you;
  Straight in our faces you burned your brand,
  Marking your chosen ones, young, young land.

When did we long for the sheltered gloom
  Of the older game with its cautious odds?
Gloried we always in sun and room,
  Spending our strength like the younger gods.
By the wild, sweet ardor that ran in us,
By the pain that tested the man in us,
  By the shadowy springs and the glaring sand,
  You were our true-love, young, young land.

When the last free trail is a prim, fenced lane
  And our graves grow weeds through forgetful
      Mays,
Richer and statelier then you 'll reign,
  Mother of men whom the world will praise.
And your sons will love you and sigh for you,
Labor and battle and die for you,
  But never the fondest will understand
  The way we have loved you, young, young land.

TRAIL'S END

'Tween the old times and the new,
I have sung heart songs of you —
You, lean stranger to all fear,
Careless border cavalier.

Now, old pard, that you are gone,
And the gray and cheerless dawn
Of a day called Progress comes,
And the throaty engine hums
Down the trail where you and I
Made our camps and watched the sky
Drop its crimson sunset bars
To a bunch of mav'rick stars —
Then, oh then, I cry aloud
Curses on the white-faced crowd,
On the heights of stone and wood,
Standing where our line-camps stood;
On the jangle of the street,
And each pale, worn face I meet.
On the coyote ways of men —
Sharp of fang beyond our ken —

Snapping o'er a brother's bones
For a pile of yellow stones.
Did we seek for gold or fame?
No, we played a careless game;
And on plunging ponies we
Shouted back in mocking glee,
When in town the black gun spoke
Through a smiling wreath of smoke.

Thus I dream and long and fret,
For my heart will not forget —
Not forget those old, red days
Of the trail — its careless ways;
Not forget — you know the sign —
Answer me, O pard of mine.

THE WESTERNER

My fathers sleep on the sunrise plains,
And each one sleeps alone.
Their trails may dim to the grass and rains,
For I choose to make my own.
I lay proud claim to their blood and name,
But I lean on no dead kin;
My name is mine, for the praise or scorn,
And the world began when I was born
And the world is mine to win.

They built high towns on their old log sills,
Where the great, slow rivers gleamed,
But with new, live rock from the savage hills
I'll build as they only dreamed.
The smoke scarce dies where the trail-camp lies,

Till the rails glint down the pass;
The desert springs into fruit and wheat
And I lay the stones of a solid street
Over yesterday's untrod grass.

I waste no thought on my neighbor's birth
Or the way he makes his prayer.
I grant him a white man's room on earth
If his game is only square.
While he plays it straight I'll call him mate;
If he cheats I drop him flat.
Old class and rank are a wornout lie,
For all clean men are as good as I,
And a king is only that.

I dream no dreams of a nurse-maid state
That will spoon me out my food.
A stout heart sings in the fray with fate
And the shock and sweat are good.
From noon to noon all the earthly boon
That I ask my God to spare
Is a little daily bread in store,
With the room to fight the strong for more,
And the weak shall get their share.

The sunrise plains are a tender haze
And the sunset seas are gray,
But I stand here, where the bright skies blaze
Over me and the big to-day.
What good to me is a vague " maybe "
Or a mournful " might-have-been,"
For the sun wheels swift from morn to morn
And the world began when I was born —
And the world is mine to win.

THE HORSEBACK FARMER

When a feller 's been a cowman, this farmin' stunt
    comes tough;
  It ain't that he 's afraid of work or weather,
But this walkin' in the furrow is a leetle mite too
    rough,
  He 'd rather take his seat in saddle-leather;
When he tackles irrigatin' and must open up a ditch,
  Does he don hip-boots and spring in with elation?
No, he takes his gentlest pony, that will neither
    prance nor pitch
  And he shovels from a horseback elevation.

When he goes to fix the wind-mill he saddles up a
    horse,
  Though it ain't a hundred yards he 'd have to
    toddle;
If he starts to feed the critters he must don his
    spurs of course,
  This walking he can't quite get in his noddle.
He rides to do the milking and he rides to fix the
    fence,
  And he rides to lock or liberate the chickens;
If he could n't find a bronco he would never hasten
    hence,
  For he says all foot-work hurts him like the
    dickens.

When a feller 's been a cowman he can't plod
    around the place
  Jest like a chap that 's never herded cattle;

He 's got to have a pony or he 'd feel he 's in dis-
    grace;
  A horseman, he, in life's eternal battle.
And when he strikes a pasture where there ain't
    a fence in sight,
  Down where the ancient cattle trail was branchin,'
He 'll spend an hour in dreamin' — he 's a hope-
    less case all right,
  This cowman who has tackled punkin' ranchin'.

SLEEPIN' OUT

Once let a feller git in tune
  With all outdoors, there hain't no use
Fer him to think he kin ferget,
  Or from the wild's big ways jar loose.
He 's always thinkin' 'bout them nights —
  Jes' listen now, and hear him sigh,
A-dreamin' of an old tarp bed,
  And sleepin' out beneath the sky.

There hain't no bunk in any house,
  That to the warm earth kin compare;
She 's sort o' kind and comfortin',
  And gives you strength as you lie there.
And then, besides, you gulp all night
  The clean, sweet air; and in the morn
There hain't a doubt or fear but what
  Your rested soul jes' laughs to scorn.

Go, take your little, stuffy room,
  Yer four walls that corral you in;

Pull down the curtain, then git up
  Chuckful o' meanness, and begin
The day with grouch and grunt and groan;
  Be civilized and right in style;
While them who rest beneath the stars
  Rise with a whoop, and smile and smile.

HIGH-CHIN BOB

'Way high up in the Mokiones, among the moun-
    tain tops,
  A lion cleaned a yearlin's bones and licked his
    thankful chops,
When who upon the scene should ride a-trippin'
    down the slope,
  But High-Chin Bob of sinful pride and maverick-
    hungry rope.

" Oh, Glory be to me! " says Bob, " and Fame's
    unfadin' flowers.
  I ride my good top-hoss to-day, and I 'm top
    hand of Lazy-J,
So kitty-cat, you 're ours! "

That lion licked his paws so brown and dreamed
    soft dreams of veal,
  As High-Chin's loop come circlin' down and
    roped him round his meal;
He yowled quick fury to the world and all the hills
    yelled back;
  That top-hoss give a snort and whirled and Bob
    caught up the slack;

" Oh, Glory be to me! " says he, " and to my glory
     trail;
   No man has looped a lion's head and lived to drag
     the bugger dead,
'Til I shall tell the tale."

'Way high up in the Mokiones that top-hoss done
     his best,
   'Mid whippin' brush and rattlin' stones from
     canyon-floor to crest;
Up and down and round and cross, Bob pounded,
     weak and wan,
   But pride still glued him to his hoss and glory
     druv him on.

" Oh, Glory be to me," says he, " this glory trail is
     rough,
   But I 'll keep this dally round the horn until the
     toot of Judgment morn
Before I 'll holler ' Nuff.' "

Three suns had rode their circle home beyond the
     desert's rim,
   And turned their star-herds loose to roam the
     ranges high and dim,
But every time Bob turned and hoped the limp re-
     mains to find,
   A red-eyed lion, belly-roped, but healthy, loped
     behind.

" Oh, Glory be to me," says Bob, " he can't be
     drug to death;
   These heroes that I 've read about, were only
     fools who stuck it out,
'Til the end of mortal breath."

'Way high up in the Mokiones, if you ever camp
    there at night,
  You 'll hear a ruckus 'mongst the stones that 'll
    lift your hair with fright.
You 'll see a cow-hoss thunder by and a lion trail
    along,
  While the rider bold with chin on high sings
    forth his glory-song!

" Oh, Glory be to me," says he, " and to my
    mighty noose;
  Oh, pardner, tell my friends below I took a ragin'
    dream in tow,
And though I never laid him low — I never turned
    him loose! "

"WALK, DAMN YOU, WALK!"

Up the dusty way from Frisco town,
  To where the mines their treasures hide,
The road is long and many miles
  The golden store and town divide.

Along this road, one summer day
  There toiled a tired man;
Begrimed with dust, the weary way
  He cussed as some folks can.

Our traveler hailed a passing team
  That slowly dragged its load along;
His hail roused up the teamster old
  And checked his jolly song.

" Say, stranger ! "

"Wa'l, whoa ! "

"Kin I walk
      Behind yer load
      A spell on this road ? "

" Wa'l, no, ye can't walk;
      But git up on this seat,
      An' we 'll jest talk.
      Git up hyar ! "

" That ain't what I want;
      I ain't that kind;
      Fer it 's on behind,
   Right in yer dust,
      That 's like a smudge,
      I want to trudge,
   Fer I desarve it ! "

" Wa'l, pard, I ain't no hog;
   I don't own this road afore nor 'hind,
So jest git right in the dirt and walk,
   If that 's the way yer 'clined ! "

" Yeh, hup ! gelang ! " the driver said;
   The creeping wagon moved amain;
While close behind the stranger toiled,
   And clouds of dust rose up again.

The teamster heard the stranger talk,
   As if two trudged behind his van;
Yet, looking round, could only spy
   A solitary man.

Yet heard the teamster words like these,
  Come out the dust as from a cloud;
For the weary footman spoke his mind,
  His thoughts he uttered loud.

And this the burden of his talk:
  " Walk now, damn you, walk!
    No use to talk;
    Don't like it, eh?
    Not the way
      Ye went at Frisco?
    Walk, damn you, walk!

  " Went up in the mines,
     An' made yer stake;
     'Nough to take
    Ye back to the state
    Where ye wuz born;
    Where now is yer corn?
     Walk, damn you, walk!

  " Dust in yer eyes,
     Dust in yer nose,
    Dust down yer throat,
     An' thick on yer clothes;
    Can't hardly talk.
     I know it! But you jest
    Walk, damn you, walk!

  " Wot did ye do with yer tin?
    Oh, blowed every ounce of it in!
    Got drunk, got sober, got drunk ag'in.
     Wa'l, walk, damn you, walk!

" Wot did ye do? Wa'l, I sw'ar
When ye was down thar,
  Tell me wot ye did n't do?
  Yer gold-dust flew;
Ye thought it fine
To keep a-openin' wine.
  Now walk, damn you, walk!

" Every one wuz yer friend,
When ye had the dust to spend
And the coin fer to lend —
Did n't think of the end;
  Tried to buck a queer game —
  Nary a red, now, to yer name.
Wa'l, walk, damn you, walk!

" Had a cool forty thousand or so.
Now wot ye got to show
  Fer all that?
Not a cussed red cent.
Ye let her went —
  Nothin' too good
  Fer yer youthful blood.
Now walk, damn you, walk!

" Chokes ye, this dust?
Wa'l, that ain't the wust —
  When ye git thar,
  Where the diggin's are,
No pick, no shovel, no pan!
Wa'l, ye 're a healthy man —
  Jest walk, damn you, walk!

" Wisht ye could stop to drink —
   What? Water? Wa'l, jest think
      How, at Frisco — wa'l, water thar
      With ye, wa'nt anywhar —
   It was wine — Extra Dry!
   Oh, you flew high!
      Now walk, damn you, walk!

" Ye say ye 've somethin' larned?
   Wa'l, I be darned!
      Hearn ye say that afore;
      Yet ye tried — jest onct more.

" Wa'l, that 's so; but this is the last!
   I 'm done! Jig 's up! All 's past!
      Ye hear me talk?
      Walk, damn you, walk!

" I 've sworn off."
                        " Guess ye 're late."
" No more on my plate.
      If I ag'in git my pile —
      Wa'l, I should smile!
         Let me ag'in salt her down,
         I 'll go round that Frisco town,
      If I walk —
         Yes, damn me, walk! "

.   .   .   .

The fools don't all go to Frisco town;
Nor do they all from the mines come down.
About all of us have, in our day,
In some sort of shape, some kind of way,

Painted the town with the " old stuff "
Dipped in stocks or made some bluff;
Got caught in wedlock by a shrew;
Mixed wines, old and new;
Seen the sights, been out all night,
Rolled home in the morning light,
With crumpled shirt and went to bed,
Waked up at noon with an awful head;
    Then how we walked, Hell! how we walked!

Now don't try to yank every bun;
Don't try to have *all* the fun;
  Don't think you know it all;
  Don't know that stocks will fall;
Don't try to bluff on an ace;
Don't know *the* horse in the race;
Don't get scooped by a pretty face;
  Lest when you awake,
    You may talk,
  And the burden be,
    " Walk, damn you, walk! "

IN DEFENCE OF THE BUSH

So you're back from up the country, Mr. Towns-
    man, where you went,
And you're cursing all the business in a bitter dis-
    content;
Well, we grieve to disappoint you, and it makes us
    sad to hear
That it was n't cool and shady — and there was n't
    plenty beer,

And the loony bullock snorted when you first came
    into view;
Well, you know it's not so often that he sees a swell
    like you;
And the roads were hot and dusty, and the plains
    were burnt and brown,
And no doubt you're better suited drinking lemon
    squash in town.

Yet, perchance, if you should journey down the very
    track you went
In a month or two at furthest you would wonder
    what it meant;
Where the sunbaked earth was gasping like a crea-
    ture in its pain
You would find the grasses waving like a field of
    summer grain,
And the miles of thirsty gutters blocked with sand
    and choked with mud —
You would find them mighty rivers with a turbid,
    sweeping flood;
For the rain and drought and sunshine make no
    changes in the street,
In the sullen line of buildings and the ceaseless
    tramp of feet;
But the bush hath moods and changes, as the sea-
    sons rise and fall,
And the men who know the bush-land — they are
    loyal through it all.

.   .   .   .

But you found the place was dismal and a land of
    no delight —
Did you chance to hear a chorus in the shearers'
    huts at night?

Did they "rise up William Riley" by the camp-fire's
　　cheery blaze?

Did they rise him as we rose him in the good old
　　droving days?

And the women of the homesteads and the men you
　　chanced to meet —

Were their faces sour and saddened like the "faces
　　in the street"?

And the "shy selector children" — were they better
　　now or worse

Than the little city urchins who would greet you with
　　a curse?

Is not such a life much better than the squalid street
　　and square

Where the fallen women flaunt it in the fierce elec-
　　tric glare?

Where the sempstress plies her sewing till her eyes
　　are sore and red

In a filthy, dirty attic toiling on for daily bread?

Did you hear no sweeter voices in the music of the
　　bush

Than the roar of trams and 'buses and the war-
　　whoop of "the push"?

Did the magpies rouse your slumbers with their
　　carol sweet and strange?

Did you hear the silver chiming of the bell-birds on
　　the range?

But, perchance, the wild birds' music by your senses
　　was despised,

For you say you'll stay in townships till the bush is
　　civilized.

Would you make it a tea-garden and on Sundays
    have a band
Where the "blokes" might take their "donahs,"
    with a "public" close at hand?
You had better stick to Sydney and make merry
    with "the push,"
For the bush will never suit you and you'll never
    suit the bush.

DRINKING SONG

When Horace wrote his noble verse,
    His brilliant, glowing line,
He must have gone to bed the worse
    For good Falernian wine.
No poet yet could praise the rose
In verse that so serenely flows
Unless he dipped his Roman nose
    In good Falernian wine.

    Shakespeare and Jonson, too,
    Drank deep of barley brew —
    Drank deep of barley brew, my boys,
    Drank deep of barley brew!

When Alexander led his men
    Against the Persian King,
He broached a hundred hogsheads, then
    They drank like anything.
They drank by day, they drank by night,
And when they marshaled for the fight,
Each put a score of foes to flight —
    Then drank like anything!

No warrior worth his salt
But quaffs the mighty malt —
But quaffs the mighty malt, my boys,
But quaffs the mighty malt !

When Patrick into Ireland went
  The works of God to do,
It was his excellent intent
  To teach men how to brew.
The holy saint had in his train
A man of splendid heart and brain —
A brewer was this worthy swain —
  To teach men how to brew.

The snakes he drove away
Were teetotalers, they say —
Teetotalers, they say, my boys,
Teetotalers, they say !

SUCCESS

If you want a thing bad enough
To go out and fight for it,
Work day and night for it,
Give up your time and your peace and your sleep
      for it —
If only desire of it
Makes you quite mad enough
Never to tire of it,
Makes you hold all other things tawdry and cheap
      for it —
If life seems all empty and useless without it,
And all that you scheme and you dream is about it,

If gladly you'll sweat for it,
Fret for it,
Plan for it,
Lose all your terror of God or man for it,
With all your capacity,
Strength and sagacity,
Faith, hope and confidence, stern pertinacity —
If neither cold poverty, famished and gaunt,
Nor sickness nor pain,
Of body or brain,
Can turn you away from the thing that you want —
If dogged and grim you besiege and beset it —
      You'll get it!

THE BOYS WHO NEVER GREW UP

THE FOREIGN LEGION

If the bowl be of gold and the liquor of flame,
  What if poison lie in the cup?
If the maiden be fair — our soul's in the game,
If her kisses be death, we'll kiss just the same,
  Sang the Legion of Boys Who Never Grew Up.

Blind with the blindness of youth, but with all
    of it
  Clearer of vision than seers! The refrain
"France is beset!" smote their ears and the call
    of it
  Woke the boy-dreamers from Nippon to Spain.
Boers from the Veldt and Hidalgos from Aragon,
  Cowmen from Argentine, Yankees from Maine,
Race of the Cæsars from Venice to Taragon
  Rallied to France to play soldier again.

Under the Tri-Color, long khaki files of them,
　　Through the Étoile, down the Champs Élysées
Marched, while grisettes blew their kisses to
　　　　miles of them,
　　And only the old brushed the tear-stains away . . .
Out where the crows spread their ominous pinions
　　Shadowing France from Nancy to Fay,
Singing they marched 'gainst the Kaiser's grey
　　　　minions —
　　Singing the song of Boyhood at play . . .

If the bowl be of gold and the liquor of flame,
　　What if poison lie in the cup?
If the maiden be fair — our soul 's in the game . . .
If her kisses be death — we 'll kiss just the
　　　　same . . .
　　Sang the Legion of Boys Who Will Never Grow
　　Up.

PLAY THE GAME!

There 's a breathless hush in the Close to-night —
　　Ten to make and the match to win —
A bumping pitch and a blinding light,
　　An hour to play and the last man in.
And it 's not for the sake of a ribboned coat
　　Or the selfish hope of a season's fame,
But his Captain's hand on his shoulder smote;
　　" Play up! Play up! And play the game! "

The sand of the desert is sodden red —
　　Red with the wreck of a square that broke;
The Gatling 's jammed and the colonel dead,
　　And the regiment 's blind with dust and smoke.

The river of death has brimmed his banks,
   And England 's far and Honor a name,
But the voice of a schoolboy rallies the ranks,
   " Play up! Play up! And play the game!"

This is the word that year by year,
   While in her place the School is set,
Every one of her sons must hear,
   And none that hears it dare forget.
This they all with a joyful mind
   Bear through life like a torch in flame,
And falling, fling to the host behind —
   " Play up! Play up! And play the game!"

THE REVEL

EAST INDIA

We meet 'neath the sounding rafter,
And the walls around are bare;
As they shout back our peals of laughter
It seems that the dead are there.
Then stand to your glasses, steady!
We drink to our comrades' eyes:
One cup to the dead already —
Hurrah for the next that dies!

Not here are the goblets glowing,
Not here is the vintage sweet;
'T is cold, as our hearts are growing,
And dark as the doom we meet.
But stand to your glasses, steady!
And soon shall our pulses rise:
A cup to the dead already —
Hurrah for the next that dies!

There 's many a hand that 's shaking,
And many a cheek that 's sunk;
But soon, though our hearts are breaking,
They 'll burn with the wine we 've drunk.
Then stand to your glasses, steady!
'T is here the revival lies:
Quaff a cup to the dead already —
Hurrah for the next that dies!

Time was when we laughed at others;
We thought we were wiser then;
Ha! Ha! let them think of their mothers,
Who hope to see them again.
No! stand to your glasses, steady!
The thoughtless is here the wise:
One cup to the dead already —
Hurrah for the next that dies!

Not a sigh for the lot that darkles,
Not a tear for the friends that sink;
We 'll fall 'midst the wine cup's sparkles,
As mute as the wine we drink.
Come, stand to your glasses, steady!
'T is this that the respite buys:
A cup to the dead already —
Hurrah for the next that dies!

There 's a mist on the glass congealing,
'T is the hurricane's sultry breath;
And thus does the warmth of feeling
Turn ice in the grasp of death.
But stand to your glasses, steady!
For a moment the vapor flies:

Quaff a cup to the dead already —
Hurrah for the next that dies!

Who dreads to the dust returning?
Who shrinks from the sable shore,
Where the high and haughty yearning
Of the soul can sting no more?
No — stand to your glasses, steady!
The world is a world of lies;
A cup to the dead already —
And hurrah for the next that dies!

Cut off from the land that bore us,
Betrayed by the land we find,
When the brightest have gone before us,
And the dullest are most behind —
Stand, stand to your glasses, steady!
'T is all we have left to prize:
One cup to the dead already —
Hurrah for the next that dies!

THE CONQUEST OF THE AIR

With a thunder-driven heart
  And the shimmer of new wings,
I, a worm that was, upstart;
  King of kings!

I have heard the singing stars,
  I have watched the sunset die,
As I burst the lucent bars
  Of the sky.

Lo, the argosies of Spain
    As they ploughed the naked brine,
Found no heaven-girded main
    Like to mine.

Soaring from the clinging sod,
    First and foremost of my race,
I have met the hosts of God
    Face to face:

Met the tempest and the gale
    Where the white moon-riven cloud
Wrapt the splendor of my sail
    In a shroud.

Where the ghost of winter fled
    Swift I followed with the snow,
Like a silver arrow sped
    From a bow.

I have trailed the summer south
    Like a flash of burnished gold,
When she fled the hungry mouth
    Of the cold.

I have dogged the ranging sun
    Till the world became a scroll;
All the oceans, one by one,
    Were my goal.

Other wingéd men may come,
    Pierce the heavens, chart the sky,
Sound an echo to my drum
    Ere they die.

I alone have seen the earth,
 Age-old fetters swept aside,
In the glory of new birth —
 Deified!

THE AIRMAN'S BATTLE HYMN

Up and upward, soaring, soaring,
 Lift our battle to the skies!
In this world of light the roaring
 Of the temporal tumult dies.
Winged from time, we strive together;
 Past the wind's last wave we run,
Climbing up the gleaming weather
 Toward the radiance of the sun!

Swung afar, your guns have spoken:
 Little flecks of white between
Lie like wool on blue unbroken
 O'er the earth — a mist of green.
Round and round, and sunward ever,
 You the lustrous, aye the free,
Lured to death by life's endeavor,
 Soaring 'mid immensity.

Winged at length, the royal ranger
 Beats his passage through the skies!
Man from danger unto danger
 Fares beyondward, wanton wise,
Seeks a goal through all betiding,
 Flings the void his fleeting breath,
And with rapture riding, riding,
 Takes the starry way to death!

Earth beneath us, planet o'er us,
    Wheeling, wheeling out of view;
Constellations speed in chorus
    As we circle, I and you,
Lone 'mid grand creation's story,
    Through the vastness not a cry,
Poised for battle in the glory,
    We are seraphs ere we die!

Past the toils of time our flight is;
    In the proud ascent we plod,
Where the heights' unattained light is
    Breathless in the gaze of God.
Here our quarrel and our questing
    End — but nearer to the sun.
Sternly at the last the testing
    Comes to all that man hath won.

Brave men strove and died before us,
    But we strive in fields profound,
Far above the star that bore us,
    In the vastness not a sound.
Only here your shell-bursts under
    Spread and fall like fiery rain.
With the gun smoke's silver wonder
    Idle on an azure plain.

Nearer to the sun, my foemen!
    I above, and you below,
Swung o'er the abyss, where no men
    Venture, neither tempests blow,
Silent . . . Poising in the splendor,
    Passionate with mortal breath.

Sweeps my soul, with no surrender,
   Down the deep to you — and death!

Ruin kissed, but gamesome ever,
   Proud we meet amid the blue;
Who shall speed the world's endeavor,
   Splendid foemen, I or you?
Here we crash; the great downcasting
   Waits. May weal us all betide!
Buoyant with the everlasting,
   Lords of death, we ride — we ride!

THE GREY HORSE TROOP

All alone on the hillside
Larry and Barry and me;
Nothin' to see but the sky and the plain,
Nothin' to see but the drivin' rain,
Nothin' to see but the painted Sioux,
Galloping, galloping, "Whoop — Whuroo!
The divil in yellow is down in the mud!"
Sez Larry to Barry, "I 'm losin' blood."

"Cheer for the Greys!" yells Barry;
"Second Dragoons!" groans Larry;
"Hurrah! Hurrah! for Egan's Grey Troop!
Whoop! ye divils, ye 've got to whoop;
Cheer for the troopers who die," sez I —
"Cheer for the troop that never shall die!"

All alone on the hillside,
Larry and Barry and me;
Flat on our bellies and pourin' in lead —
Seven rounds left and the horses dead —

Barry a-cursin' at every breath;
Larry beside him as white as death;
Indians galloping, galloping by,
Wheelin' and squealin' like hawks in the sky!

" Cheer for the Greys! " yells Barry;
" Second Dragoons! " groans Larry;
" Hurrah! Hurrah! for Egan's Grey Troop!
Whoop, ye divils — ye 've got to whoop;
Cheer for the troopers who die," sez I —
" Cheer for the troop that never shall die! "

All alone on the hillside,
Larry and Barry and me;
Two of us livin' and one of us dead —
Shot in the head, and God, how he bled!
" Larry 's done up," sez Barry to me;
" Divvy his cartridges! Quick! Gimme three! "
While nearer and nearer and plainer in view
Galloped and galloped the murderin' Sioux.

" Cheer for the Greys! " yells Barry;
" Cheer — " and he falls on Larry.
Alas! Alas! for Egan's Grey Troop!
The red Sioux hovering, stoop to swoop;
Two out of three lay dead, while I
Cheered for the troop that never shall die.

All alone on the hillside,
Larry and Barry and me;
And I fired and yelled and lost my head,
Cheerin' the livin', cheerin' the dead,

Swingin' my cap I cheered until
I stumbled and fell. Then over the hill
There floated a trumpeter's silvery call,
And Egan's Grey Troop galloped up. That 's all.

Drink to the Greys and Barry!
Second Dragoons — and Larry!
Here 's a bumper to Egan's Grey Troop!
Let the crape on the guidons droop;
Drink to the troopers who die; while I
Drink to the troop that never shall die.

THE LION'S CUB

The whelp that nipped its mother's dug in turning
    from her breast,
And smacked its lusty lips and built its own lair in
    the West,
Has stretched its limbs and looked about and
    roared across the sea;
"Oh, mother I did bite thee hard, but still thou
    lovest me!"

She lifts her head and listens, as waking from a
    dream,
Her great jaws set, her claws outspread, her lion
    eyes agleam;
The voice is deep as thunder on the far horizon rim,
And thus the mother spoke and said: "It can be
    none but him!"

Cried England to America; "My ancient love
    abides,
And the old Trafalgar courage still upon the ocean
    rides."

America to England spake; " The God of Liberty
Goes with us marching up the land and sailing down
the sea."

And the twain are joined for hunting—let all the
packs beware,
The tiger's kith, the panther's kin, the race-
hordes of the bear.
They two step forth together, God's hand has
struck the hour,
All pathways lead to freedom, each footstep
broadens power.

The world is still in dull amaze, agape and dazed
to hear;
There is a rustling of the thrones, uneasy far and
near,
King leaning unto king and on Oppression's hate-
ful lips
A pallor as the winds bring in the booming of the
ships.

And who shall cower, who recoil, or choose the
craven's tack,
And strain the law (by heroes made) to hold his
country back?
Ah, who? Let children lisp his shame and women
cry him down
What time our glorious banner waves o'er stormèd
tower and town.

The star is up, the star of splendor, never to set or
wane;
The flag leads on, the flag of glory, never to turn
again;

And where it goes we cheer and follow, no man of
us will fail;
We all are where our armies camp and where our
navies sail.

World-conquering mother, hard we bit in parting
from thy breast;
Yet still we smack our lusty lips and love thy milk
the best;
For the blood our mother gave us is the true, im-
perial strain;
She bore one cub, one only, but it wears the lion's
mane!

THE RIDERLESS HORSE

Close ranks and ride on!
　Though his saddle be bare,
The bullet is sped,
　Now the dead cannot care.

Close ranks and ride on!
　Let the pitiless stride
Of the host that he led
Though his saddle be red,
　Sweep on like the tide.

Close ranks and ride on!
　The banner he bore
For God and the right
　Never faltered before.

Quick, up with it, then!
For the right! For the right!
Lest legions of men
Be lost in the night!

R.N.V.R.

When it is ended how shall I return
And gather up the raveled threads again
Of my past life — content once more to earn
My daily bread in drudgery and pain?
I — that have been one of the fellowship
Of those who dare the dangers of the sea
And know the lift and swing of a big ship
Surging, full-power, to action under me.

I — that have heard shells scream and seen men
die
Laughing, as if the war were but a game;
And known the lust of battle; seen the sky
Filled, end to end, with whirling sheets of
flame.
And felt my veins, long coursed by sluggish blood,
Now thrilled and filled with wine and molten
fire;
These have I known and I have found them good.
Can I to any lesser heights aspire?

I — that have seen Aurora's pallid spears
Defiantly shaken in the face of Heaven
And felt that thrill of beauty, close to tears,
That flowers deep in the heart when, low at ev'n,

Out of the Western sky of palest green
   When all the sea is hushed and tremulous,
That first bright star gleams forth, pure, pale,
     serene,
   Touching the waves with silver — Hesperus?

I — that have seen God's fingers paint the dawn
   In bars of rose and flame upon the East
And watched the night-mists as a veil withdrawn
   Fretted with gold and pearl and amethyst —
I — that have seen the hill-high, smoking surge,
   Burst at our bows in rainbow-tinted spray
And heard the taut shrouds moaning like a dirge —
   Can I go back to smoky towns and gray?

With dirty streets and sordid offices
   And stupid talk in trains with stupid men —
Oh, every rustle of the dusty trees
   Will bring remembrance and regret and pain.
I 'll think I hear the whisper as the bow
   Shears deep into the phosphorescent sea
And lifting, drips pale fire and green. Oh how
   Can life be ever as before to me?

And will your kiss delight me as of old,
   Whose lips have felt the sea's salt, fierce caress?
Or, shall I find your love-making grown cold,
   And wearisome your talk and tenderness?
And long and long for the gray, open sea
   And the untainted wind upon my mouth,
To know again the infinite, deep peace
   Healing my soul like cool rain after drouth?

THE HELL-GATE OF SOISSONS

My name is Darino, the poet. You have heard?
    Oui, Comédie Française.
Perchance it has happened, *mon ami,* you know of
    my unworthy lays.
Ah, then you must guess how my fingers are itch-
    ing to talk to a pen;
For I was at Soissons, and saw it, the death of
    twelve Englishmen.

My leg, *malheureusement!* I left it behind on the
    banks of the Aisne.
Regret? I would pay with the other to witness their
    valor again.
A trifle, indeed, I assure you, to give for the honor
    to tell
How that handful of British, undaunted, went into
    the gateway of Hell.

Let me draw you a plan of the battle. Here, we
    French and your Engineers stood;
Over there a detachment of German sharpshooters
    lay hid in a wood.
A *mitrailleuse* battery planted on top of this well-
    chosen ridge
Held the road for the Prussians and covered the
    direct approach to the bridge.

It was madness to dare the dense murder that
    spewed from those ghastly machines.
(Only those who have danced to its music can know
    what the *mitrailleuse* means.)

But the bridge on the Aisne was a menace; our
    safety demanded its fall;
" Engineers, — volunteers!" In a body, the Royals
    stood out at the call.

Death at best was the fate of that mission — to their
    glory no one was dismayed.
A party was chosen and seven survived till the
    powder was laid.
And *they* died with their fuses unlighted. Another
    detachment! Again
A sortie is made — all too vainly. The bridge still
    commanded the Aisne.

We were fighting two foes — Time and Prussia —
    the moments were worth more than troops.
We *must* blow up the bridge. A lone soldier darts
    out from the Royals and swoops
For the fuse! Fate seems with us. We cheer him;
    he answers; our hopes are newborn!
A ball rips his visor — his khaki shows red where
    another has torn.

Will he live? Will he last? Will he make it? *Hélas!*
    and so near to the goal —
A second; he dies! then a third one! A fourth!
    Still the Germans take toll!
A fifth! *Magnifique!* It is magic! How does he
    escape them? He may . . .
Yes, he does! See, the match flares! A rifle rings
    out from the wood and says, " Nay! "

Six, seven, eight, nine, take their places; six, seven,
    eight, nine brave their hail;
Six, seven, eight, nine — how we count them! but
    the sixth, seventh, eighth and ninth fail.
A tenth! *Sacre nom!* But these English are sol-
    diers — they know how to try;
(He fumbles the place where his jaw was) — they
    show, too, how heroes can die.

Ten we count — ten who ventured unquailing —
    ten there were — and ten are no more!
Yet another salutes and superbly essays where the
    ten failed before.
God of Battles, look down and protect him! Lord,
    his heart is as Thine — let him live!
But the *mitrailleuse* splutters and stutters and rid-
    dles him into a sieve.

Then I thought of my sins and sat waiting the
    charge that we could not withstand;
And I thought of my beautiful Paris, and gave a
    last look at the land,
At France, *ma belle France* in her glory of blue sky
    and green field and wood,
Death with honor but never surrender. And to die
    with such men — it was good.

They are forming — the bugles are blaring —
    they will cross in a moment and then . . .
When out of the line of the Royals (your island,
    mon ami, breeds men)

Burst a private — a tawny-haired giant, it was
    hopeless but, *ciel!* how he ran!
Bon Dieu, please remember the pattern and make
    many more on the plan!

No cheers from our ranks, and the Germans, they
    halted in wonderment too;
See, he reaches the bridge; ah! he lights it! I am
    dreaming, it *cannot* be true.
Scream of rage! Fusillade! They have killed him!
    Too late though; the good work is done.
By the valor of twelve English martyrs the Hell-
    Gate of Soissons is won!

HIS SHARE

" I 'ave bought me a bit o' ground,
    And I think I 'll rest
Out o' the sight and the sound
    O' what I 've knowed best.

" I 'ave come to my small estate
    Through a many o' seas;
I 'ave wrought wi' the weak and the great,
    Forgettin' my ease.

" I 'ave paid for my own free'old
    In coin o' worth;
I 'ave striven wi' strong men and bold
    For my piece o' Earth.

  .   .   .   .

" I 'ave bought me a bit o' ground
    Wi' blood and pain,

And I 'm come, wi' my dyin' wound,
Back to England again.

" My free'old is six feet long,
And may be as deep.
I 've bought it, and not for a song —
I think — I 'll sleep."

I HAVE A RENDEZVOUS WITH DEATH

I have a rendezvous with Death
At some disputed barricade,
When Spring comes back with rustling shade
And apple-blossoms fill the air —
I have a rendezvous with Death
When Spring brings back blue days and fair.

It may be he shall take my hand
And lead me into his dark land
And close my eyes and quench my breath —
It may be I shall pass him still.
I have a rendezvous with Death
On some scarred slope of battered hill,
When Spring comes round again this year
And the first meadow-flowers appear.

God knows 't were better to be deep
Pillowed in silk and scented down,
Where Love throbs out in blissful sleep,
Pulse nigh to pulse, and breath to breath,
Where hushed awakenings are dear . . .
But I 've a rendezvous with Death

At midnight in some flaming town,
When Spring trips north again this year,
And I to my pledged word am true,
I shall not fail that rendezvous.

INVICTUS

Out of the night that covers me,
  Black as the Pit from pole to pole,
I thank whatever gods may be
  For my unconquerable soul.

In the fell clutch of circumstance
  I have not winced nor cried aloud,
Beneath the bludgeonings of chance
  My head is bloody but unbowed.

Beyond this place of wrath and tears
  Looms but the Horror of the shade —
And yet the menace of the years
  Finds and shall find me unafraid.

It matters not how strait the gate,
  How charged with punishments the scroll
I am the master of my fate:
  I am the captain of my soul.

THE MONK

I go with silent feet and slow
As all my black-robed brothers go;
I dig awhile and read and pray,
So portion out my pious day

Until the evening-time and then
Work at my book with cunning pen.

If *she* should turn to me and smile —
My book would be no more to me
Than some forgotten phantasy,
And God no more unto my mind
Than a dead leaf upon the wind.

THE SONG OF BROTHER HILARIO

Oh, a godly man on a goodly plan,
  With an ample girth, am I.
I love my food as a hale man should,
  And a vintage old and dry.
I do what 's right, as the right I see,
  And I rise up when I fall;
And in things that are too high for me
  I meddle me not at all!

For Hilario shall come and go,
  As to-morrow and to-day;
But the kind am I that shall live and die,
  And be glad he passed this way!

I like a book by the ingle nook,
  With a pipe and mulled old ale;
To crack a jest of a piquant zest,
  If it be not over stale!
Yet an ancient tale, if it be well told,
  From its ashes still can rise;
And a simple song, be it moss-grown old,
  Is a thing that never dies!

I like to dream by the quiet stream,
  Where the simple waters flow.
I love the knell of the vesper bell,
  When the sinking sun lies low.
I like to think, when my day is dead,
  And the night falls dark and deep,
That this sweet earth shall be my bed,
  When I lay me down to sleep!

For Hilario shall come and go,
  As to-morrow and to-day;
But the kind am I that shall live and die,
  And be glad he passed this way!

GIFTS

Give a man a horse he can ride,
Give a man a boat he can sail:
And his rank and wealth, his strength and health
On sea nor shore shall fail.

Give a man a pipe he can smoke,
Give a man a book he can read:
And his home is bright with a calm delight,
Though his room be poor indeed.

Give a man a girl he can love,
As I, O my love, love thee:
And his heart is great with the pulse of Fate,
At home, on land, on sea.

FALSTAFF'S SONG

Where 's he that died o' Wednesday?
  What place on earth hath he?
A tailor's yard beneath, I wot,
  Where worms approaching be;
For the wight that died o' Wednesday,
  Just laid the light below,
Is dead as the varlet turned to clay
  A score of years ago.

Where 's he that died o' Sabba' day?
  Good Lord, I 'd not be he!
The best of days is foul enough
  From this world's fare to flee;
And the saint that died o' Sabba' day,
  With his grave turf yet to grow,
Is dead as the sinner brought to pray
  A hundred years years ago.

Where 's he that died o' yesterday?
  What better chance hath he
To clink the can and toss the pot
  When this night's junkets be?
For the lad that died o' yesterday
  Is just as dead — ho! ho! —
As the whoreson knave men laid away
  A thousand years ago.

LAZARUS

Still he lingers, where wealth and fashion
  Meet together to dine or play,
Lingers, a matter of vague compassion,
  Out in the darkness across the way;

Out beyond the warmth and the glitter,
 And the light where luxury's laughter rings,
Lazarus waits, where the wind is bitter,
 Receiving his evil things.

Still you find him, when breathless, burning
 Summer flames upon square and street,
When the fortunate ones of the earth are turning
 Their thoughts to meadows and meadowsweet;
For far away from the wide green valley,
 And the bramble patch where the whitethroat
    sings,
Lazarus sweats in his crowded alley,
 Receiving his evil things.

And all the time from a thousand rostrums
 Wise men preach upon him and his woes,
Each with his bundle of noisy nostrums
 Torn to tatters 'twixt ayes and noes;
Sage and Socialist, gush and glamour,
 Yet little relief their wisdom brings,
For there's nothing for him out of all the clamor,
 Nothing but evil things.

Royal commissions, creeds, convictions,
 Learnedly argue and write and speak,
But the happy issue of his afflictions,
 Lazarus waits for it week by week.
Still he sees it to-day, to-morrow,
 In purposeless pavement wanderings,
Or dreams it, a huddled heap of sorrow,
 Receiving his evil things.

And some will tell you of evolution
   With social science thereto; and some
Look forth to the parable's retribution,
   When the lot is changed in the life to come,
To the trumpet sound and the great awaking,
   To One with healing upon His wings
In the house of the many mansions making,
     An end of the evil things.

In the name of Knowledge the race grows healthier,
   In the name of Freedom the world grows great,
And men are wiser, and men are wealthier,
   But — Lazarus lies at the rich man's gate;
Lies as he lay through human history,
   Through fame of heroes and pomp of kings —
At the rich man's gate, an abiding mystery,
     Receiving his evil things.

"DOMINUS ILLUMINATIO MEA"

In the hour of death, after this life's whim,
When the heart beats low and the eyes grow dim,
And pain has exhausted every limb —
   The lover of the Lord shall trust in Him.

When the will has forgotten the lifelong aim,
And the mind can only disgrace its fame,
And a man is uncertain of his own name —
   The power of the Lord shall fill this frame.

When the last sigh is heaved, and the last tear shed,
And the coffin is waiting beside the bed,

And the widow and child forsake the dead —
The angel of the Lord shall lift this head.

For even the purest delight may pall,
And power must fail, and the pride must fall,
And the love of the dearest friends grow small —
But the glory of the Lord is all in all.

TO HIS MOTHER, C. L. M.

In the dark womb where I began
My mother's life made me a man.
Through all the months of human birth
Her beauty fed my common earth.
I cannot see, nor breathe, nor stir
But through the death of some of her.

Down in the darkness of the grave
She cannot see the life she gave.
For all her love, she cannot tell
Whether I use it ill or well,
Nor knock at dusty doors to find
Her beauty dusty in the mind.

If the grave's gates would be undone,
She would not know her little son,
I am so grown. If we should meet,
She would pass by me in the street,
Unless my soul's face let her see
My sense of what she did for me.

What have I done to keep in mind
My debt to her and womankind?

What woman's happier life repays
Her for those months of wretched days?
For all my mouthless body leech'd
Ere Birth's releasing hell was reach'd?

What have I done, or tried, or said
In thanks to that dear woman dead?
Men triumph over women still,
Men trample women's rights at will,
And men's lust roves the world untamed,

   .   .   .   .

O grave, keep shut lest I be shamed!

THE SWIMMER

With short, sharp, violent lights made vivid,
  To southward far as the sight can roam;
Only the swirl of the surges livid,
  The seas that climb and the surfs that comb.
Only the crag and the cliff to nor'ward,
And the rocks receding, and the reefs flung for-
    ward,
And waifs wreck'd seaward and wasted shoreward
  On shallows sheeted with flaming foam.

A grim grey coast and a seaboard ghastly,
  And shores trod seldom by feet of men —
Where the batter'd hull and the broken mast lie,
  They have lain embedded these long years ten.
Love! when we wander'd here together,
Hand in hand through the sparkling weather,
From the heights and hollows of fern and heather,
  God surely loved us a little then.

The skies were fairer and shores were firmer —
   The blue sea over the bright sand roll'd;
Babble and prattle, and ripple and murmur,
   Sheen of silver and glamour of gold —
And the sunset bath'd in the gulf to lend her
A garland of pinks and of purples tender,
A tinge of the sun-god's rosy splendour,
   A tithe of his glories manifold.

Man's works are graven, cunning, and skilful
   On earth where his tabernacles are;
But the sea is wanton, the sea is wilful,
   And who shall mend her and who shall mar?
Shall we carve success or record disaster
On the bosom of her heaving alabaster?
Will her purple pulse beat fainter or faster
   For fallen sparrow or fallen star?

I would that with sleepy soft embraces
   The sea would fold me — would find me rest
In luminous shades of her secret places,
   In depths where her marvels are manifest,
So the earth beneath her should not discover
My hidden couch — nor the heaven above her —
As a strong love shielding a weary lover,
   I would have her shield me with shining breast.

When light in the realms of space lay hidden,
   When life was yet in the womb of time,
Ere flesh was fettered to fruits forbidden,
   And souls were wedded to care and crime,
Was the course foreshaped for the future spirit —
A burden of folly, a void of merit —

That would fain the wisdom of stars inherit,
  And cannot fathom the seas sublime?

Under the sea or the soil (what matter?
  The sea and the soil are under the sun),
As in the former days in the latter,
  The sleeping or waking is known of none,
Surely the sleeper shall not awaken
To griefs forgotten or joys forsaken,
For the price of all things given and taken,
  The sum of all things done and undone.

Shall we count offences or coin excuses,
  Or weigh with scales the soul of a man,
Whom a strong hand binds and a sure hand looses
  Whose light is a spark and his life a span?
The seed he sowed or the soil he cumber'd,
The time he served or the space he slumber'd;
Will it profit a man when his days are number'd,
  Or his deeds since the days of his life began?

One, glad because of the light, saith, " Shall not
  The righteous Judge of all the earth do right,
For behold the sparrows on the house-tops fall not
  Save as seemeth to Him good in His sight? "
And this man's joy shall have no abiding
Through lights departing and lives dividing,
He is soon as one in the darkness hiding,
  One loving darkness rather than light.

A little season of love and laughter,
  Of light and life, and pleasure and pain,

And a horror of outer darkness after,
  And dust returneth to dust again.
Then the lesser life shall be as the greater,
And the lover of life shall join the hater,
And the one thing cometh sooner or later,
  And no one knoweth the loss or gain.

Love of my life! we had lights in season —
  Hard to part from, harder to keep —
We had strength to labour and souls to reason,
  And seed to scatter and fruits to reap.
Though time estranges and fate disperses,
We have had our loves and our loving — mercies;
Though the gifts of the light in the end are curses,
  Yet bides the gift of the darkness — sleep!

See! girt with tempest and wing'd with thunder,
  And clad with lightning and shod with sleet,
The strong winds treading the swift waves sunder
  The flying rollers with frothy feet.
One gleam like a bloodshot sword blade swims on
The skyline, staining the green gulf crimson,
A death stroke fiercely dealt by a dim sun
  That strikes through his stormy winding sheet.

Oh, brave white horses! you gather and gallop,
  The storm sprite loosens the gusty reins;
Now the stoutest ship were the frailest shallop
  In your hollow backs, or your high-arch'd manes.
I would ride as never a man has ridden
In your sleepy, swirling surges hidden,
To gulfs foreshadow'd through straits forbidden,
  Where no light wearies and no love wanes.

SEA FEVER

I must go down to the seas again, to the lonely sea
    and the sky,
And all I ask is a tall ship and a star to steer her by,
And the wheel's kick and the wind's song and the
    white sail's shaking,
And a grey mist on the sea's face and a grey dawn
    breaking.

I must go down to the seas again, for the call of
    the running tide
Is a wild call and a clear call that may not be denied;
And all I ask is a windy day with the white clouds
    flying,
And the flung spray and the brown spume, and the
    sea-gulls crying.

I must go down to the seas again to the vagrant
    gypsy life,
To the gull's way and the whale's way where the
    wind 's like a whetted knife;
And all I ask is a merry yarn from a laughing fel-
    low-rover,
And quiet sleep and a sweet dream when the long
    trick 's over.

HASTINGS MILL

As I went down by Hastings Mill I lingered in my
    going
To smell the smell of piled-up deals and feel the
    salt wind blowing,

To hear the cables fret and creak and the ropes
    stir and sigh
(Shipmate, my shipmate!) as in days gone by.

As I went down by Hastings Mill I saw a ship there
    lying,
About her tawny yards the little clouds of sunset
    flying,
And half I took her for the ghost of one I used to
    know
(Shipmate, my shipmate!) many years ago.

As I went down by Hastings Mill I saw while I
    stood dreaming
The flicker of her riding light along the ripples
    streaming,
The bollards where we made her fast and the berth
    where she did lie
(Shipmate, oh shipmate!) in the days gone by.

As I went down by Hastings Mill I heard a fellow
    singing,
Chipping off the deep-sea rust above the tide a-
    swinging;
And well I knew the queer old tune and well the
    song he sung
(Shipmate, my shipmate!) when the world was
    young.

And past the rowdy Union Wharf, and by the still
    tide sleeping,
To a randy-dandy deep-sea tune my heart in time
    was keeping,

To the thin far sound of a shadowy watch a-haul-
ing,
And the voice of one I knew across the high tide
calling
(Shipmate, my shipmate!) and the late dusk falling.

THE RECALL

An ancient ghost came up the way —
The western way, the windy way —
Across a world of land and sea,
With greeting from afar to me:

" Hast thou forgot the open way,
The winding way, the wandering way,
With freedom of strong sun and rain
To clear the roving heart of pain?

" Yet still the long roads greet the sun,
And glad wayfarers one by one
Follow the gold day down the west
That once made part of thy unrest.

" Hast thou forgot the ocean way,
The wondrous way, the thundrous way,
The fierce enchantment of the sea,
The memory, the mystery?

" Yet still the tall ships gather home
From tropic worlds beyond the foam;
And still the outbound steamers go
Down foreign seas thou once didst know.

" Hast thou forgot the forest way,
   The shady way, the silent way,
   The thin, blue camp-smoke in the dawn,
   The brave, bright fires when night came on ?

" Still the free forest glooms and shines
   With moonlight on the silvered pines,
   Although by hill and lonely shore
   Their noiseless trails know thee no more."

   So came an ancient ghost to me,
   Idling beside a winter sea,
   The lost familiar of my breast,
   The spirit of the old unrest.

THE SEA GIPSY

   I am fevered with the sunset,
     I am fretful with the bay,
   For the wander-thirst is on me
     And my soul is in Cathay.

   There 's a schooner in the offing
     With her topsails shot with fire,
   And my heart has gone aboard her
     For the Islands of Desire.

   I must forth again to-morrow,
     With the sunset I must be,
   Hull down on the trail of rapture
     In the wonder of the sea.

THE PORT O' HEART'S DESIRE

Down around the quay they lie, the ships that sail to
 sea,
On shore the brown-cheeked sailormen they pass
 the jest with me;
But soon their ships will sail away with winds that
 never tire,
And there 's one that will be sailing to the Port o'
 Heart's Desire.

The Port o' Heart's Desire, and it 's, oh, that port
 for me,
And that 's the ship that I love best of all that sail
 the sea;
Its hold is filled with memories, its prow it points
 away
To the Port o' Heart's Desire, where I roamed a
 boy at play.

Ships that sail for gold there be, and ships that sail
 for fame,
And some were filled with jewels bright when from
 Cathay they came;
But give me still yon white sail in the sunset's
 mystic fire,
That the running tides will carry to the Port o'
 Heart's Desire.

It 's you may have the gold and fame, and all the
 jewels, too,
And all the ships, if they were mine, I 'd gladly give
 to you;

I 'd give them all right gladly, with their gold and
  fame entire,
If you would set me down within the Port o' Heart's
  Desire.

Oh, speed you, white-winged ships of mine, oh,
  speed you to the sea,
Some other day, some other tide, come back again
  for me;
Come back with all the memories, the joys and
  e'en the pain,
And take me to the golden hills of boyhood once
  again.

WARNING

When the old moon hangs to the cloud's gray tail
  And the stars play in and out;
When the East grows red and the West looks pale
  And the wind goes knocking about;

When over the edge of the shapeless coast,
  Where the horizon bites the cloud,
The rack of the rain stalks in like a ghost
  And a sail blows through its shroud —

When the morn is such, of the noon beware!
  For this calm's a stormy feint:
A reef in the sail is better than prayer,
  For a snug ship needs no saint.

ON THE QUAY

I 've never traveled for more 'n a day,
I never was one to roam,
But I likes to sit on the busy quay,
Watchin' the ships that says to me —
" Always somebody goin' away,
Somebody gettin' home."

I likes to think that the world 's so wide —
'T is grand to be livin' there,
Takin' a part in its goin's on . . .
Ah, now ye 're laughin' at poor old John,
Talkin' o' works o' the world wi' pride
As if he was doin' his share!

But laugh if ye will! when ye 're old as me
Ye 'll find 't is a rare good plan
To look at the world — and love it, too! —
Though never a job are ye fit to do . . .
Oh 't is n't all sorrow and pain to see
The work o' another man.

'T is good when the heart grows big at last,
Too big for trouble to fill —
Wi' room for the things that was only stuff
When workin' an' winnin' seemed more 'n enough —
Room for the world, the world so vast,
Wi' its peoples an' all their skill.

That 's what I 'm thinkin' on all the days
I 'm loafin' an' smokin' here,

An' the ships do make me think the most
(Of readin' in books 't is little I 'd boast), —
But the ships they carries me long, long ways,
An' draws far places near.

I sees the things that a sailor brings,
I hears the stories he tells . . .
'T is surely a wonderful world, indeed!
'T is more 'n the peoples can ever need!
An' I praises the Lord — to myself I sings —
For the world in which I dwells.

An' I loves the ships more every day
Though I never was one to roam.
Oh! the ships is comfortin' sights to see,
An' they means a lot when they says to me —
" Always somebody goin' away,
Somebody gettin' home."

PORTRAIT OF AN OLD SEA CAPTAIN

Varras, the painter, had him in to pose,
An ancient Gloucesterman whose course was run,
A man who marked each going of the sun
As who should see another doorway close
Upon his hope, and know that hope was done.

Varras was twenty-seven. He had found
A cottage impudently near the sea.
Its rooms were filled with the ocean sound,
Its windows gave the sense of being free,

So much they held of the distant blue and gold.
Varras and I were young . . . but the Gloucester-
    man was old.

He sat in the model's place
With a patch of sunlight on his withered cheek
(As though a rose should touch a dead man's face) —
And Varras painted him . . . I did not speak,
So thralled I was with watching that swift birth
And dawn of careless color! Shortly, eyes
Looked from the canvas, and their light was worth
A long day's tramp to see! What precious skies
He broke and plundered for those daubs of blue
I know not, but I know that heaven lay
Behind them, and a kindled star or two
And the laid fire of another day.
It was not youth, but courage to be old
That he had caught from those dim flickering
    gleams —
"I 'll put my picture in a frame of gold ! "
Said Varras, and brushed his own eyes of their
    dreams.

The Gloucesterman got slowly from his chair,
Looked at the portrait, long and wonderingly,
Then straightened his bent form and turned to
    stare
Through the clear window to the sapphire sea,
"I never thought to make another trip,"
He said. " But Lord, I 'm only eighty odd;
I 'll die in open water yet, please God —
Once more . . . to be the master of a ship!

What 's in your art to make an old man brag?"
He asked, and wheeled on Varras, but that youth,
Having created something more than truth,
Was cleaning brushes with a paint-smeared rag.

THE MAIN-SHEET SONG

Rushing along on a narrow reach,
  Our rival under the lee,
The wind falls foul of the weather leach,
  And the jib flaps fretfully.
The skipper casts a glance along,
  And handles his wheel to meet —
Then sings in the voice of a stormy song,
  "All hands get on that sheet!"

Yo ho! Yo ho! Then give her a spill,
  With a rattle of blocks abaft.
Yo ho! Yo ho! Come down with a will
  And bring the main-sheet aft.

Rolling the foam up over the rail
  She smokes along and flings
A spurt of spray in the curving sail,
  And plunges and rolls and springs;
For a wild, wet spot is the scuppers' sweep,
  As we stand to our knees along —
It's a foot to make and a foot to keep
  As we surge to the bullie's song.

Yo ho! Yo ho! Then give her a spill,
  With a rattle of blocks abaft.
Yo ho! Yo ho! Come down with a will
  And bring the main-sheet aft.

Muscle and mind are a winning pair
  With a lively plank below,
That whether the wind be foul or fair
  Will pick up her heels and go;
For old hemp and hands are shipmates long —
  There's work whenever they meet —
So here's to a pull that's steady and strong,
  When all hands get on the sheet.

Yo ho! Yo ho! Then give her a spill
  With a rattle of blocks abaft,
Yo ho! Yo ho! Come down with a will
  And bring the main-sheet aft.

WEST INDIA DOCK ROAD

Black man, white man, brown man, yellow man,
  All the lousy Orient loafing on the quay;
Hindoo, Dago, Jap, Malay and Chinaman
  Dipping into London from the great green sea!

Black man, white man, brown man, yellow man,
  Pennyfields and Poplar and Chinatown for me!
Stately moving cutthroats and many colored mys-
    teries;
  Never were such lusty things for London days to
    see!

On the evil twilight, rose and star and silver,
  Steals a song that long ago in Singapore they
    sang;
Fragrant of spices, of incense and opium,
  Cinnamon and aconite, the betel and the bhang.

Three miles straight lies lily-clad Belgravia,
　Thin-lipped ladies and padded men and pale.
But here are turbaned princes and velvet-glancing
　　gentlemen,
　Tomtom and shark knife and salt-caked sail.

Then get you down to Limehouse, by rigging, wharf
　　and smokestack,
　Glamour, dirt and perfume, and dusky men and
　　gold;
For down in lurking Limehouse there's the blue
　　moon of the Orient,
　Lamps for young Aladdins and bowies for the
　　bold!

DERELICT

"The Dead Man's Chest," as is known to exceeding few,
is the name of a treacherous sunken reef in the Caribbean
Sea. The legend upon which Mr. Allison has based his
remarkable poem is to the effect that during that flourish-
ing period of piracy on the "Spanish Main" in the seven-
teenth century, a Spanish galleon, returning home heavily
laden with treasure, was raided by a piratical crew who
made every man-jack aboard the galleon walk the plank
and then fell to fighting among themselves over the divi-
sion of the loot. The result of this "free for all" was that
fifteen husky cutthroats set their less powerful compan-
ions adrift in the long boat with just enough fresh water
and sea-biscuit to last them until they reached the main-
land. The fifteen worthies left in possession of the gal-
leon and its treasure, being no better able to agree among
themselves as to its division than their luckless com-
panions whom they had abandoned, in turn started a
fight among themselves which resulted in the death of all.
The galleon drifted derelict on the Dead Man's Chest,
where she was subsequently discovered by those mem-

bers of the crew who had been set adrift. And — it is the
bo's'n's mate who tells the story of the sight which met
their eyes as they clambered up the side. — R. F.

Fifteen men on the Dead Man's Chest —
Drink and the devil had done for the rest —
　　The mate was fixed by the bo's'n's pike,
　　The bo's'n brained with a marlinspike,
　　And Cookey's throat was marked belike
　　　　It had been gripped
　　　　　By fingers ten;
　　　　And there they lay,
　　　　　All good, dead men,
Like break-o'-day in a boozing ken —
　　Yo-ho-ho and a bottle of rum!

Fifteen men of a whole ship's list —
Dead and be-damned and the rest gone whist! —
　　The skipper lay with his nob in gore
　　Where the scullion's axe his cheek had shore —
　　And the scullion he was stabbed times four.
　　　　And there they lay,
　　　　　And the soggy skies
　　　　Dripped all day long
　　　　　In up-staring eyes —
At murk sunset and at foul sunrise —
　　Yo-ho-ho and a bottle of rum!

Fifteen men of 'em stiff and stark —
Ten of the crew had the murder mark —
　　'T was a cutlass swipe, or an ounce of lead,
　　Or a yawing hole in a battered head, —
　　And the scuppers glut with a rotting red.

And there they lay —
    Aye, damn my eyes! —
All lookouts clapped
    On paradise —
All souls bound just contrariwise —
    Yo-ho-ho and a bottle of rum!

Fifteen men of 'em good and true —
Every man-jack could ha' sailed with Old Pew —
    There was chest on chest full of Spanish gold,
    With a ton of plate in the middle hold,
    And the cabins, riot of loot untold.
        And they lay there
            That had took the plum,
        With sightless glare
            And their lips struck dumb,
While we shared all by the rule of thumb —
    Yo-ho-ho and a bottle of rum!

More was seen through the sternlight screen —
Chartings ondoubt where a woman had been —
    A flimsy shift on a bunker cot,
    With a thin dirk slot through the bosom-spot,
    And the lace stiff-dry in a purplish blot . . .
        Or was she wench,
            Or some shuddering maid
        That dared the knife
            And that took the blade?
By God! She was stuff for a plucky jade;
    Yo-ho-ho and a bottle of rum!

Fifteen men on the Dead Man's Chest —
Drink and the devil had done for the rest —

We wrapped 'em all in a mains'l tight,
With twice ten turns of a hawser's bight,
And we heaved 'em over and out of sight —
    With a yo-heave-ho!
    And a fare-you-well!
    And a sullen plunge
    In the sullen swell,
Ten fathoms deep on the road to hell!
Yo-ho-ho and a bottle of rum!

SHIPMATES

Good-bye, and fare ye well, for we'll sail no more
    together
Broad seas and narrow in fair and foul weather;
We'll sail no more together in foul weather or
    fine,
And ye'll go your own way and I'll go mine.

Oh, the seas are very wide, and there's never any
    knowing
The countries we'll see or the ports where we'll be
    going;
All across the wide world, up and down the sea,
Before we come together, as at last may be.

Good-bye and fare ye well; and maybe I'll be stroll-
    ing,
And watching the ships there and the crews a-coal-
    ing,
In a queer foreign city and a gay, gaudy street —
And who but yourself will I chance there for to
    meet?

You'll blow up from Eastward and I'll blow in from
 West,
And of all the time we ever had it's then we'll have
 the best.
Back from deep-sea wanderings, back from wind
 and weather,
You and me from all the seas, two friends together!

Good-bye and fare ye well. May naught but good
 attend ye
All across the wide world where sailor's luck may
 send ye —
Up and down the deep seas, north and south the
 Line,
And ye'll go your own way and I'll go mine!

THE COASTERS

Overloaded, undermanned,
  Trusting to a lee,
Playing I-spy with the land,
  Jockeying the sea —
That's the way the Coaster goes,
  Through calm and hurricane:
Everywhere the tide flows,
Everywhere the wind blows,
  From Mexico to Maine.

O East and West! O North and South!
  We ply along the shore,
From famous Fundy's foggy mouth,
  From voes of Labrador;

Through pass and strait, on sound and sea,
   From port to port we stand —
The rocks of Race fade on our lee,
   We hail the Rio Grande.
Our sails are never lost to sight;
   On every gulf and bay
They gleam, in winter wind-cloud white,
   In summer rain-cloud gray.

We hold the coast with slippery grip;
   We dare from cape to cape;
Our leaden fingers feel the dip
   And trace the channel's shape.
We sail or bide as serves the tide
   Inshore we cheat its flow,
And side by side at anchor ride
   When stormy head-winds blow.
We are the offspring of the shoal,
   The hucksters of the sea;
From customs theft and pilot toll
   Thank God that we are free.

Legging on and off the beach,
   Drifting up the strait,
Fluking down the river reach,
   Towing through the gate —
That's the way the Coaster goes,
   Flirting with the gale:
Everywhere the tide flows,
Everywhere the wind blows,
   From York to Beavertail.

Here and there to get a load,
   Freighting anything;

Running off with spanker stowed,
  Loafing wing-a-wing —
That's the way the Coaster goes,
  Chumming with the land:
Everywhere the tide flows,
Everywhere the wind blows,
  From Ray to Rio Grande.

We split the swell where rings the bell
  On many a shallow's edge,
We take our flight past many a light
  That guards the deadly ledge;
We greet Montauk across the foam,
  We work the Vineyard Sound,
The Diamond sees us running home,
  The Georges outward bound;
Absecon hears our canvas beat
  When tacked off Brigantine;
We raise the Gulls with lifted sheet,
  Pass wing-and-wing between.

Off Monomoy we fight the gale,
  We drift off Sandy Key;
The watch of Fenwick sees our sail
  Scud for Henlopen's lee,
With decks awash and canvas torn
  We wallow up the Stream;
We drag dismasted, cargo borne,
  And fright the ships of steam.
Death grips us with his frosty hands
  In calm and hurricane;
We spill our bones on fifty sands
  From Mexico to Maine.

Cargo reef in main and fore,
   Manned by half a crew,
Romping up the weather shore,
   Edging down the Blue —
That's the way the Coaster goes,
   Scouting with the lead:
Everywhere the tide flows,
Everywhere the wind blows,
   From Cruz to Quoddy Head.

THE NEW ROUTE

Oh, we have known the gales that blow
   About the Polar Sea,
And battled racing tides that flow
   And combers rolling free.
We 've fought the winds that roar so raw
   And chill men to the core;
But now we go by Panama —
   We 'll round the Horn no more!
       No more!
We 'll round the Horn no more,
And bones of good men shall not bleach
   Upon that cruel shore.
Past Colon town we shape our course.
   We 'll round the Horn no more!

The storms came shrieking from the Pole,
   The ice floes clogged our course,
And on our beam-ends we would roll
   Beneath the tempest's force.
That was a voyage meant for men —
   Stout-hearted men of yore;

But we 'll not brave that course again —
  We 'll round the Horn no more!
        No more!
We 'll round the Horn no more,
But loiter through the calm Canal
  That cuts from shore to shore,
And rob the breakers of their prey.
  We 'll round the Horn no more!

Oh, you who follow after us
  Shall take the better way,
Nor try the passage perilous
  We ventured in our day.
Yet we are glad that we have known
  The perils that we bore,
And thank our stars that day has flown —
  We 'll round the Horn no more!
        No more!
We 'll round the Horn no more,
And bones of good men shall not bleach
  Upon that iron shore;
For now we go by Panama.
  We 'll round the Horn no more!

THE DECKHANDS

There 's some is bums from city slums
That ain't so strong on knowledge;
There 's some that hails from county jails
An' some that hails from college;
There 's some is mild an' some is wild
An' some is smart an' chipper —
The kind that climbs an' gets, sometimes,
To be a mate or skipper.

A lousy lot
You 'll say, an' not
What you 'd consider what is what;
Well, yes, we lack
A high shellac
But we 're not meant for bric-à-brac.

Believe me, pard, we 're rough and hard
An' scarcely things of beauty;
We 're never made for dress parade
But just for heavy duty;
To strain our spines at handlin' lines —
To do our stint of swabbin' —
When combers roll to pass the coal
To keep the screws a-throbbin'.

It 's true we ain't
Exactly " quaint "
Like " hale old salts " the painters paint,
But we can do
The work for you—
An' that 's the business of a crew.

We 're single guys without no ties
Of any kind to bind us,
Tho' I can't state the aggregate
Of girls we 've left behind us.
In port we drink an' get in " clink "
In spite of ev'ry warnin' —
Our money spent, we 're all content
To ship again next mornin'.

The mate may rare
An' swear an' tear —
Us deckhands does n't greatly care,

For kicks an' blame
Is in the game —
They 've got to have us just the same.

November blows an' wintry snows
Don't find us any glummer,
We still can shirk our daily work
As well as in the summer.
For, so we gets our cigarettes
An' wages, when it 's over
We 'll take a trip in any ship
An' think ourselves in clover.

We would n't please
At balls or teas,
Where high-toned folks is what you sees;
But don't you doubt
This fact, old scout,
We 're guys they can't get on without.

THE SAILOR OF THE SAIL

I sing the Sailor of the Sail — breed of the oaken
        heart,
Who drew the world together and spread our race
        apart,

Whose conquests are the measure of thrice the
        ocean's girth,
Whose trophies are the nations that necklace half
        the earth.

Lord of the Bunt and Gasket and Master of the
     Yard,
To whom no land was distant, to whom no sea was
     barred:

Who battled with the current, who conquered with
     the wind,
Who shaped the course before him by the wake he
     threw behind;

Who burned in twenty climates; who froze in twenty
     seas,
Who crept the shore of Labrador and flash'd the
     Caribbees;

Who followed Drake, who fought with Blake, who
     broke the bar of Spain,
And who gave to timid traffic the freedom of the
     main;

Who woke the East, who won the West, who made
     the North his own,
Who weft his wake in many a fake athwart the
     Southern zone;

Who drew the thread of commerce through Sun-
     da's rocky strait,
Who faced the fierce Levanter where England holds
     the gate;

Who saw the frozen mountains draw down the
     moonlike sun;
Who felt the gale tear at the sail and ice gnaw at the
     run:

Who drove the lance of barter through Asia's an-
     cient shield,
Who tore from drowsy China what China dare not
     yield;

Who searched with Cook, beholding him unroll be-
     neath his hand
The last, the strangest continent, the sundered
     Southern land;

To whom all things were barter — slaves, spices,
     gold, and gum;
Who gave his life for glory, who sold his soul for
     rum —

I sing him, and I see him, as only those can see
Who stake their lives to fathom that solveless
     mystery;

Who on the space of waters have fought the killing
     gale,
Have heard the crying of the spar, the moaning of
     the sail;

Who never see the ocean but that they feel its
     hand
Clutch like a siren at the heart to drag it from the
     land.

I see him in the running when seas would over-
     whelm,
Lay breathing hard along the yard and sweating at
     the helm.

I see him at the earing light out the stubborn
    bands
When every foot of canvas is screeved with bloody
    hands.

I see him freezing, starving — I see him scurvy
    curst,
Alone, and slowly dying, locked in the hell of thirst.

I see him drunk and fighting roll through some sea-
    board town,
When those who own and rob him take to the street
    and frown.

O Sovereign of the Boundless! O Bondsman of the
    Wave!
Who made the world dependent, yet lived and died
    a slave —

In Britain's vast Valhalla, where sleep her worst
    and best —
Where lies the grave she made you — your first
    and final rest —

Beneath no stone or trophy, beneath no minster
    tower,
Lie those who gave her Empire, who stretched her
    arm to power.

Below those markless pathways where commerce
    shapes the trail,
Unsung, unrung, forgotten, sleeps the Sailor of the
    Sail.

ADMIRALS ALL

Effingham, Grenville, Raleigh, Drake,
  Here's to the bold and free!
Benbow, Collingwood, Byron, Blake,
  Hail to the Kings of the Sea!
Admirals all, for England's sake,
  Honour be yours and fame!
And honour, as long as waves shall break,
  To Nelson's peerless name!

Essex was fretting in Cadiz Bay
  With the galleons fair in sight;
Howard at last must give him his way,
  And the word was passed to fight.
Never was schoolboy gayer than he,
  Since holidays first began:
He tossed his bonnet to wind and sea,
  And under the guns he ran.

Drake nor devil nor Spaniard feared,
  Their cities he put to the sack;
He singed his Catholic Majesty's beard,
  And harried his ships to wrack.
He was playing at Plymouth a rubber of bowls
  When the great Armada came;
But he said, " They must wait their turn, good
    souls,"
  And he stooped, and finished the game.

Fifteen sail were the Dutchmen bold,
  Duncan he had but two:
But he anchored them fast where the Texel shoaled,
  And his colours aloft he flew.

" I 've taken the depth to a fathom," he cried,
    " And I 'll sink with a right good will:
For I know when we 're all of us under the tide,
    My flag will be fluttering still."

Splinters were flying above, below,
    When Nelson sailed the Sound:
" Mark you, I would n't be elsewhere now,"
    Said he, " for a thousand pound! "
The Admiral's signal bade him fly,
    But he wickedly wagged his head,
He clapped his glass to his sightless eye
    And " I 'm damned if I see it," he said.

Admirals all, they said their say
    (The echoes are ringing still),
Admirals all, they went their way
    To the haven under the hill.
But they left us a kingdom none can take,
    The realm of the circling sea,
To be ruled by the rightful sons of Blake
    And the Rodneys yet to be.

BEYOND THE PATH OF THE OUTMOST SUN

Beyond the path of the outmost sun, through utter
        darkness hurled
Further than ever comet flared or vagrant stardust
        swirled —
Live such as fought and sailed and ruled and loved
        and made our world.

They are purged of pride because they died, they
    know the worth of their bays;
They sit at wine with the Maidens Nine and the
    Gods of the Elder Days.
It is their will to serve or be still as fitteth our
    Father's praise.

It is theirs to slip through the ringing deep where
    Azrael's outposts are
Or buffet a path through the Pit's red wrath when
    God goes out to war,
Or hang with the reckless Seraphim on the rim
    of a red-maned star.

They take their mirth in the joy of the Earth —
    they dare not grieve for her pain —
They know of toil and the end of toil, they know
    God's law is plain,
So they whistle the Devil to make them sport who
    know that sin is vain.

And ofttimes cometh our wise Lord God, master
    of every trade,
And tells them tales of his daily toil, of Edens
    newly made;
And they rise to their feet as he passes by, gentle-
    men unafraid.

To those who are cleansed of past Desire, Sorrow
    and Lust and Shame —
Gods, for they knew the hearts of men — men, for
    they stooped to Fame,
Borne on the breath that men call Death, my
    brother's spirit came.

He scarcely had need to doff his pride or slough
    the dross of Earth —
E'en as he trod that day to God so walked he from
    his birth,
In simpleness and gentleness and honour and clean
    mirth.

So cup to lip in fellowship they gave him welcome
    high
And made him praise at the banquet board — the
    strong men ranged thereby,
Who had done his work and held his peace and
    had no fear to die.

Beyond the loom of the last lone star through open
    darkness hurled,
Further than rebel comet dared or hiving star-
    swarm swirled,
Sits he with those that praise our God for that they
    served His world.

WHAT DO YOU WANT AT SIXTY-THREE?

I live and breathe, I eat and drink,
I write and read and think I think,
I keep old friends, I wear old clothes,
I laugh at cares and have no foes —
    What do you want at sixty-three?

I love the truth, I hate all lies,
I shirk a man with downcast eyes.
I tilt at shams with all my might,
And only death will end the fight —
    What do you want at sixty-three?

I trust all men, but sometimes find
A skunk with cankered soul and mind.
That skunk and I go different ways —
    That 's what I do at sixty-three.

THIS MY LIFE

I strive to keep me in the sun;
I pick no quarrel with the years,
Nor with the Fates, not ev'n the one
That holds the shears.

I take occasion by the hand;
I 'm not too nice 'twixt weed and flower;
I do not stay to understand —
I take mine hour.

The time is short enough at best.
I push right onward while I may;
I open to the winds my breast —
And walk the way.

A kind heart greets me here and there;
I hide from it my doubts and fears.
I trudge, and say the path is fair
Along the years.

" FAME IS A FOOD THAT DEAD MEN EAT "

Fame is a food that dead men eat, —
I have no stomach for such meat.
In little light and narrow room,
They eat it in the silent tomb,

With no kind voice of comrade near
To bid the banquet be of cheer.

But Friendship is a nobler thing, —
Of Friendship it is good to sing.
For truly, when a man shall end,
He lives in memory of his friend,
Who doth his better part recall,
And of his faults make funeral.

YOUNG AND OLD

When all the world is young, lad,
  And all the trees are green,
And every goose a swan, lad,
  And every lass a queen,
Then, hey for boot and horse, lad,
  And 'round the world away!
Young blood must have its course, lad,
  And every dog his day.

When all the world is old, lad,
  And all the trees are brown,
And all the sport is stale, lad,
  And all the wheels run down,
Creep home and take your place there,
  The spent and maimed among;
God grant you find one face there,
  You loved when all was young.

DUM VIVIMUS VIGILEMUS

Turn out more ale, turn up the light;
I will not go to bed to-night.
Of all the foes that man should dread
The first and worst one is a bed.
Friends I have had both old and young,
And ale we drank and songs we sung:
Enough you know when this is said,
That, one and all, — they died in bed.
    In bed they died and I 'll not go
    Where all my friends have perished so.
    Go you who glad would buried be,
    But not to-night a bed for me.

For me to-night no bed prepare,
But set me out my oaken chair.
And bid no other guests beside
The ghosts that shall around me glide;
In curling smoke-wreaths I shall see
A fair and gentle company.
Though silent all, rare revellers they,
Who leave you not till break of day.
    Go you who would not daylight see —
    But not to-night a bed for me:
    For I 've been born and I 've been wed —
    All of man's peril comes of bed.

And I 'll not seek — whate'er befall —
Him who unbidden comes to all.
A grewsome guest, a lean-jawed wight —
God send he do not come to-night!

But if he do, to claim his own,
He shall not find me lying prone;
But blithely, bravely sitting up,
And raising high the stirrup-cup,
    Then if you find a pipe unfilled,
    An empty chair, the brown ale spilled;
    Well may you know, though naught be said,
    That I 've been borne away to bed.

THE FRIENDSHIP

Who may not stand and take a blow,
    And straight return the buffeting,
Is worthy neither friend nor foe;
    The king is dead? Long live the king!

Who doth not proudly bear his scars,
    Earned fairly in a goodly fray,
Despised by Eros, scorned by Mars,
    Fares low upon a lonely way.

And he who doth a friend despite,
    In sudden heat, by word or pen,
Nor owns that fault, though wrong or right,
    May find no place with gentle men.

Peace were a pretty thing indeed,
    Gay garlanded at banquet board,
But serveth best the common need
    When girded with the naked sword.

May I be shut from Paradise,
    Condemned by friend and foe alike,

When reason to my heart denies
  The grace to pardon — or to strike.

Who bares his shoulder to the stroke,
  Doth some small courage there attest;
But he who does true praise evoke,
  Will clench his hand — and bare his breast.

My heart to him that lustily
  Shall take the blow and give as good;
But damned be lean Hypocrisy,
  With murder hidden in its hood.

And if we meet as foe and foe,
  God knows 't will be a goodly fight;
And if we meet as friends — I know
  That I shall be a happy wight.

THE VAGABOND GROWN OLD

So warm the lighted windows glow
Across the darkness and the snow,
The trodden road, the sodden road,
The road wherein I chose to go!

The winter skies are steely gray;
The winter stars are far away.
Light were my feet when winds were sweet,
But bitter going 's mine to-day.

Still, as I trudge, I needs must sing —
For be he vagabond or king,
A man must choose what he will lose —
And I have known the Road in Spring!

ROOSEVELT — THE LEADER

From her red veins the Mother fashioned him
In gay mood of her richest burgeoning;
No stinting made she of her treasure-house,
But moulded him to quick warm sympathies,
To valiant purposes, broad-shouldered deeds.

Into his heart she poured her flaming East,
Wine of her West, her North, her tremulous South;
Matched in him glory of a Continent,
Made him of clay and star-dust — gave him feet
And wings. Like molten flame she poured her light,
Sent him swift sight to captain our stern need,
To cleanse with laughter our too heavy air,
To take away the scorn of common things,
To give the cup of water to the dog,
To lead unspeaking children by the hand.

Like writhing spawn, like serpents of the slime,
He shook the cowardices from our hearts
And startled us to seeing; sternly he taught
The measure of true manhood, unafraid
Largely to love and valiantly to hate —
This flinger-back of creeping littleness,
This scorner of the underbrush of thought.

This was thy son, America — this man
Wrought in a furnace of thy fashioning.
Unsparingly his blade of spirit cut
Into our shams and foul hypocrisies.
This was thy son, formed from the roots of earth,
And from the lifting tree-tops — this, thy son,

Fashioned of brawny stuff, of elements
Not of perfection, but warm humanness —
No haloed saint but every inch a man,
Mixed with the lightning, thunder, with the night
    and dawn —
Of great compassion, of unpitying scorn;
With unblind eyes, seeing new paths to break,
He followed far, a burning Galahad —
This man of vision with the childlike heart!

Earth is the poorer for his passing — earth
Richer for that he stayed with us awhile;
And some uncharted star-space is come bright
With pleasure of his presence.
Eagerly he went from us, as he had lived —
Swiftly and passionately as of old;
Impatient to search out new eagle trail,
Glimpsing the far horizons, how should he
Go else than swiftly into reddening dawn?

Here on the common way was all the stuff
Whereof he built his heaven; somewhere must be
Lightness and cheer and sight of homely things —
Of pipe and dog and children at their play. . . .
Surely his kindred greet him in the halls
Of the high-hearted at some festive board
Deep in Valhalla, while a shout rings out,
A pledge of fellowship — song by the fire —
" Skoal! skoal! skoal! Our Leader has arrived!
Our Champion strong, our fearless fighting Man!"

In fine and simple manliness he grasps
Hands with heroic hands, he who had need —

" Need of the sky and business with the grass " —
And fine brave business with his fellow-men.
And with quick hands they welcome him — the hosts
Of those gone forth in battle for the Right —
In some new France to lead his Volunteers,
In some new sky to find his Flying Boy!

FINIS

INDEX OF AUTHORS

INDEX OF AUTHORS